KARATE-DŌ NYŪMON

KARATE-DŌ NYŪMON

The Master Introductory Text

Gichin Funakoshi
trans. by John Teramoto

KODANSHA INTERNATIONAL
Tokyo • New York • London

Distributed in the United States by Kodansha America, Inc.,
114 Fifth Avenue, New York, N.Y. 10011, and in the United
Kingdom and continental Europe by Kodansha Europe Ltd.,
95 Aldwych, London WC2B 4JF. Published by Kodansha International Ltd., 17-14, Otowa 1-chome, Bunkyo-ku, Tokyo 112,
and Kodansha America, Inc.
First edition, 1988
First paperback edition, 1994
   95 96 5 4 3 2

Library of Congress Cataloging-in-Publication Data

Funakoshi, Gichin, 1870–1956
  Karate-dō Nyūmon.
    Translation of: Karate-dō Nyūmon, Gichin Funakoshi.
    1. Karate. I. Title.

GV1114.3F8613   1987   796.8'153
87–45211
ISBN 4-7700-1891-6

Contents

Master Gichin Funakoshi

FOREWORD

Karate-dō Nyūmon was published in Japanese in December, 1943. The present English edition marks the first translation of this book into a foreign language.

In 1984 the Japan Karate-dō Shōtōkai held various commemorative events to celebrate the tenth anniversary of the rebuilding of its central dojo and headquarters, the Shōtōkan. In 1986, we observed the thirtieth anniversary of Master Gichin Funakoshi's death. The publication of this English edition is therefore quite timely, and I consider it a great honor to write this foreword.

It is said that in the master's youth his study and practice of karate included the learning of over one hundred different kata. As a result of years of research and investigation into these formal exercises,, the master reduced the number to fifteen traditional kata. These fifteen kata, familiar under such names as Bassai and Kankū, together with the five introductory Heian kata, form the central core of Shōtōkai training.

The kata called Ten no Kata, explained in this book, was created and designed under the leadership and guidance of Master Funakoshi. It is a kata unique to the Shōtōkai and is proudly cherished by all of us, his students.

Master Funakoshi felt that, rather than a great variety of kata, it is more important to take a limited number and practice them thoroughly and precisely. This way of thinking can be regarded as basic to the Shōtōkai.

A Japanese maxim says, *Kantan na mono yoku kachi o seisu*.'"The balance between victory and defeat often hangs on simple matters."

And another admonishes, *Shoshin o wasurezu.* "(In your training) do not forget the spirit and humility of a beginner."

This does not mean that it is sufficient to practice only basics. To accurately digest and improve even simple combat techniques and basic movements, practice of the more advanced traditional kata is utterly essential.

Unlike the advanced kata, practice in basics tends to be limited to simple forward and backward movements. The complexity of integrated left-right, forward-backward, pivoting, turning, two- and three-step advancing or retreating movements executed in rapid succession tends to be lost. One should question whether the practice of basics alone would allow one to respond to continuously changing circumstances, or whether one could effectively apply basic techniques under difficult conditions. In this sense, the traditional kata are extremely important for training the body under a variety of conditions. In kata, individual movements combined become more than their sum total. Kata practice is meant to lead to an understanding of the true value of the movements as self-defense techniques.

Nevertheless, all things have advantages and disadvantages. Often in practicing the advanced kata, students concentrate too much on the order and continuity of the movements, without considering the effectiveness of each technique. In extreme cases, they may have the illusion that they have mastered the kata by simply memorizing the order of the movements. It should be clear that, in reality, one must practice both basic techniques and advanced kata, and that the study of basics takes on a new and deeper meaning after one experiences more complex practice.

To return to Ten no Kata, it should first be noted that it is not necessarily an introductory kata and nothing more. Rather, it is meant to be both a kata and a continuous practice of basics. It is well suited to those who have practiced the traditional fifteen kata to the point where they have more or less mastered them and wish to further hone their skills.

Another important characteristic of Ten no Kata concerns the element of *maai*. Literally translated, *maai* means "(spatial) distance," but in this usage it also evokes a sense of timing, or chance. Thus, it indicates both the space and the time it takes for an opponent's fist to reach one's body. In the practice of both kata and basics, there is a tendency to forget *maai* and to become absorbed solely in the repetition of movements.

In traditional kata such as Bassai, the difference between simply executing the movements in the correct order and performing the kata while taking maai into account is immediately apparent. If one imagines a real opponent and performs the kata while thinking of maai, a blending of hard and soft, quick and slow elements appears quite naturally. Then each movement of the hands and feet takes the shortest possible route.

In actual practice, this concept seems rather difficult for students to grasp, even though its importance is pointed out and stressed. It is impossible to understand through words, and it seems as though the body refuses to cooperate. Besides being a trying experience for the student, it is source of much anguish to the instructor who wants his students to understand and develop this sense as quickly as possible.

The concept of maai can be instilled through the practice of Ten no Kata. My fervent wish as an instructor is that this will serve as an incentive to work hard on Ten no Kata, and especially on Ten no Kata Ura, the kumite portion of the kata. I think that the explanation in this section of the book will lead you to a deeper appreciation of maai, and this understanding will in turn influence the manner in which you practice the traditional kata. This is the idea upon which our system of practice is based. It should now be clear that Ten no Kata is more than an elementary kata.

The Shōtōkai kata span the hard and heavy kata of the Shōrei style and the light and fast kata of the Shōrin style. Emphasis on maai is an element common to both styles and kata should always be practiced with this in mind.

One of the subjects Master Funakoshi touches on in this book is his own masters: Azato, Itosu and Matsumura. This makes it an especially valuable document, and, not surprisingly, in his recollections of these three men, he indirectly refers to the importance of maai.

In the Shōtōkai, after acquiring a general understanding of Ten no Kata, we begin the practice of *kawashi*, or what might be called "interaction." In *kawashi* practice, you pass through your opponent's attack, in effect exchanging places with him. Unlike kumite kata, you do not catch the attack and sweep it away, nor do you step back or to the side. Instead you step in, towards the attacker, while turning (*kawasu*) your body to avoid the attack.

In practice, the distance between the attacker and defender should be about ninety centimeters, so that if the defender does not step in to avoid the attack, he will surely be struck. This is therefore real practice in maai. It is a drill in close-quarter fighting where you must quickly read your opponent's decision to attack.

In a fight, interaction is implicit—to do battle with the opponent is, so to speak, to interact with him. The kawashi of Ten no Kata practice, however, does not mean clash or conflict; on the contrary, it means to pass by or cross through one's opponent without the slightest physical contact, in other words, to interact, but not in the material realm.

In the practice of basics, this interacting is reflected quite naturally in body movements like the retraction of the left fist to the hip when punching with the right hand. Even in blocking with the sword hand, the opposite sword hand held in front of the chest is in essence a retracted pulling hand.

Karate practice reinforces the idea that before engaging in combat, you must first experience kawashi with your own self. In other words, karate is a martial art of self-examination.

In closing, I wish to say that I would be more than happy if, through this book, students could come to understand Ten no Kata as a basic training method embodying traditional concepts, such as kawashi, that have been passed down over the years. And I hope that it will help students advance in their practice of karate.

Motonobu Hironishi

PREFACE

I picture a group of us sitting cross-legged around a low table in a cozy room, sipping tea, while I answer your questions about karate. This is the image I had in mind as I wrote this book. I have tried to keep the tone light and interesting, for I wanted it to be easily readable. At the same time I did not wish to treat the subject so lightly as to be factually haphazard or careless. Indeed, one of my main purposes in writing was to correct the many false concepts about karate that have all too often been spawned by incorrect explanations and rumors. If this book enables even one person to realize the true spirit and nature of karate-dō, I would be more than grateful.

More than twenty years have passed since I first brought karate to Tokyo. Today, not only those involved in athletics and the martial arts, but also people in general have at least heard of karate. Even so, the number of individuals who really understand the true nature of karate is extremely small. Furthermore, since karate is ever advancing, it is no longer possible to speak of the karate of today and the karate of a decade ago in the same breath. Accordingly, even fewer realize that karate in Tokyo today is almost completely different in form from what was earlier practiced in Okinawa.

Dō, which signifies a "path" or "way" to polish oneself, has a life of its own, be it the *dō* of *budō*, "martial arts," or the *dō* of any of the various other arts. Precisely because it has its own life, *dō* is subject to the inevitable cycle of growth and decline. It is ever changing, but only in its outer form. The basic nature of *dō* remains immutable. If the way attracts a person to walk it, it flourishes; if not, it wastes away. The Way of karate can rightly be called a newly risen *budō* and it earnestly seeks people to walk its path.

My fondest hope is that this little book will instill in readers the desire to study karate, and that among them some will eventually come to understand the Way of karate and pass it on to others. In that event, my joy and gratitude would know no bounds.

Since this book is a basic introduction specifically for those approaching the subject for the first time, there is no room for discussing difficult theoretical questions or variations in techniques. Of the thirty-odd *kata*, "formal exercises," I have given a detailed explanation of only one, Ten no Kata. It should always be kept in mind that karate-dō cannot be grasped through eyes and ears alone; it must be experienced and comprehended through physical training. Therefore, if you take only the Ten no Kata and practice with all your heart until you master it, I can say without reservation that you will come to realize the true meaning of karate-dō.

An old proverb says, *Fugu kuwanu hito niwa iwaji.* ("It is impossible to describe the taste of blowfish to one who has never eaten it.") Similarly, the true nature of karate-dō cannot be explained in words even if one's efforts with pen or tongue are carried to the point of exhaustion and beyond.

In closing, I would like to express my deep gratitude to Messrs. Funakoshi Gigo, Hayashi Yoshiaki, and Uemura Wado for their kind assistance in compiling and editing this book.

1: KARATE POWER

In the past it was common to embellish stories about martial arts until they were just short of myths. Take, for example, the following account of an incident that was supposed to have occurred in China, long, long ago.

It was the day of a street fair, and as throngs of gaily dressed men and women filed past colorful shops and stands filled with food, cloth, toys, knickknacks and fireworks, a great commotion suddenly arose.

"A fight! It's a fight!"

"No, it's a match between those *kenpō* men again."

The crowd surged against itself. The young men eagerly rushed toward the shouting to see the fight. Screaming women and crying children frantically tried to get as far away from the trouble as possible.

At the center of the tumult stood a towering figure with a fearsome, bristling beard glinting in the sunlight and his shiny face crimson with anger and alcohol—the notorious Master Yang, drunk and the cause of trouble again. Seething with rage, he was shoving and poking a white-haired old garlic seller. Fearing for the old man's life, the crowd waited for someone to step in and rescue him, but everyone knew of Master Yang's evil temper and deaf ear for reason, so not a soul dared step forward. People chattered excitedly as they looked on, half-filled with sympathy for the poor old man, yet nonetheless curious to see what would happen next. The old man himself seemed to be completely at ease.

Tottering slightly and coughing as if he had asthma, he grinned broadly and said, "Now, your pushing me around isn't going to accomplish anything. If it's a fight you want, that's fine with me. You certainly talk big. But if talking is all that matters, anyone can be an expert. Well then, shall we begin?"

The old man coughed and stretched, looking as though he had every intention of taking on his giant opponent. The spectators were stunned.

"That old guy must be out of his mind! Doesn't he know he's up against Master Yang?"

"It doesn't look like it, does it? Otherwise he wouldn't have said what he did."

"The old man must be a stranger around here. Leastwise, I've never seen him before."

Despite Yang's unsavory reputation, he was well known as an expert in *kenpō* and a master of the spear and the staff. He had over a thousand students and was the subject of fantastic stories about his strength. Some said they had seen him knock down a runaway horse by hitting it on the nose with his fist. Others claimed he could swing and slash with a giant hundred and twenty-kilogram sword as if it were nothing and smash through a stack of ten roofing tiles with his bare hand. His arrogance and love of drink had earned him a bad name, but his great strength and skill in combat had made him feared and respected throughout the city.

The crowd was totally astounded by the old garlic vendor's response. Yang himself was surprised but it did not take long for his anger to return.

"You stupid old fool! I thought I'd spare your life, but I've changed my mind. Prepare yourself. I, Master Yang, will offer prayers over your dead body!"

With a tremendous *kiai* he thrust his fist at the old man's head. The force and fury of his attack was like a giant Deva King on a mad rampage. The crowd gasped, waiting for the punch to crush the old man's skull.

The old man moved a little to the left and stood quietly, tottering slightly as usual.

Yang, unbalanced by his own momentum, fell flat on his face. He leapt up immediately. With a frantic, terrifying look, he thrust his fist at the old man's stomach, where it struck home with a thud. Some of the onlookers covered their eyes, unable to bear the sight of the old man prostrate and vomiting blood.

But the look on the garlic vendor's face was nonchalant as he took the punch full force, and his color did not change a bit. He stood there, still tottering, with a large grin on his lips. Yang, to his consternation, found his fist still pressed against the old man's stomach. Unable to either thrust deeper or withdraw, he looked like an insect stuck to flypaper, flapping its wings, struggling to free itself. The crowd stared in bewilderment. They had never seen anything like this.

On closer inspection it could be seen that Yang's pumpkin-sized fist was caught between the folds of the old man's stomach. Master Yang, whose strength was said to be peerless, stood there sweating profusely. His fist captive, his face burning an angry red, he struggled and wriggled to no avail.

Until at last Master Yang, the drunk notorious for his arrogance, was overcome with shame. Falling to his knees, he bowed repeatedly, saying, "Master! I failed to recognize a real expert when I saw one, so I acted like a terrible fool. From now on I'll be careful and respectful to others. I humbly beg your forgiveness."

Looking at the repentant man very closely, the old man said, "If you truly understand, that's fine. You have a reputation for being an unbearable braggart. Never forget, the world is a very large place. Watch yourself, be careful about what you say and what you do."

The old man relaxed his stomach muscles and Master Yang sat down heavily. The old man walked over and picked up his sack of garlic. Coughing as he went, he left the circle of watchers and went off without so much as a backward glance.

A story like this is certainly entertaining, but problems arise when people who should know better relate such events as if they had really happened. In extreme cases, they make it sound as if they themselves had actually witnessed the occurrences.

In describing the tremendous power of karate, there are people who say such things as:

There is a secret technique in karate called *nukite* [spear hand]. With your fingertips, you can pierce the side of an adversary and grasp and extract his ribs. Training for this technique is extremely difficult. You take a forty- to fifty-liter cask filled with small beans and, holding your fingers together, begin by thrusting your fingertips into the beans. Do this ten thousand times a day. The skin will split and the fingers will bleed. Gradually the fingertips will harden and take on a grotesque appearance, but as you continue the thrusting practice, the sensation of pain will eventually disappear.

When that stage is reached, you switch from dried beans to sand. The sand will be more difficult than the beans, but after months of practice, you will be able to reach the bottom of the cask with a single thrust. Graduating from sand, you move on to gravel, to pebbles and eventually to balls of lead.

As a result of this training, you will be able to penetrate wooden boards with your fingertips, carve rocks or even pierce a horse's flank with your bare hands.

A person with no prior knowledge of karate may take such pseudo-instruction at face value and come away with the impression that karate is awesome, terrible and frightening. That this is at least partially true is attested to by such questions as, "I've heard that you know karate. Please forgive me for asking, but can you break rocks with your bare hands, or make holes in people with your fingertips?"

Faced with such an outlandish question, one should realize that the person inquiring is just an amateur. A simple smile and a straight answer, "No, I can't perform tricks like that," should do the trick. But there are always those troublesome instructors who unabashedly lead the inquirer on with replies like, "Well, I can't say that there haven't been times when I've done so . . ." Braggarts though they are, they are usually quite skillful talkers who get their listeners to believe their stories. Of course, these men may simply be thinking that through their exaggerations they are doing karate a favor by making it more attractive, that is, they are merely adding a layer of gold gilt to karate. Actually, they are covering up the true nature of karate with quite detrimental results. Isn't this like killing someone with kindness?

Besides the tale of Master Yang, the storytellers have fabricated mystical, secret techniques whose total number is limited only by their own imaginations. There may have been adepts at such techniques among the ancient masters, but I do not know a single karate master today who could perform such feats.

Again, there are instructors who mislead others with explanations of the sort, "In karate, a powerful grip is very important. In order to develop your grip, you should train by taking two jugs so wide you can barely grasp their mouths with your fingertips. Fill them with sand, hold one jug in each hand, and swing them back and forth. A person who has sufficiently developed his grip through training can rip away the flesh of an opponent's arm or leg."

Although there is some truth to the above explanation, the part about stripping away a man's flesh is ridiculous, for that's what we are talking about—human flesh, not kneaded dough. It cannot be torn so easily.

Nevertheless, one day an instructor came to my dojo and asked if I wanted him to teach me his "secret technique." I thought to myself, some men in this world do have a lot of nerve, and immediately asked him to demonstrate the technique on me. The result was nonsensical. He gave me no more than a hard pinch. Furthermore, far from stripping away my skin, his pinch did not even leave a mark. The whole matter was ludicrous.

This is not to say that a strong grip is not an advantage. I have heard of people whose power was exceedingly great. One man was able to make a complete round of the outside of his house by grabbing and swinging along from rafter to rafter. (It must be kept in mind that, unlike houses on the mainland, Okinawan houses have thicker rafters that allow for this.) And it is a fact that my respected teacher, Master Itosu, who was widely regarded as a modern-day expert in karate-dō, could crush thick bamboo stalks with his hands. I believe, however, that Itosu's grip was more a natural talent than an acquisition gained through training.

With continued training the human body can be developed to a high state of fitness and readiness. But it should always be kept in mind that there are natural limits. It is true that someone practicing karate can perform certain feats that the average person cannot, such as breaking thick boards, or smashing twelve or thirteen stacked roofing tiles. But these are things that anyone can accomplish after a little training. Board and tile breaking are really nothing more than experiments. As such, they are not essential to karate, nor are they by any stretch of the imagination secret techniques.

On the contrary, as far as karate-dō is concerned, they are extraneous elements. Often the form laymen's questions take is the curious question, "How many boards must one be able to break to earn a certain rank?" It seems that they are confusing the ranking system in karate with a ladder. [The karate rank *ichidan*, "first grade," could also mean "first rung" of a ladder.] Of course, there is no connection.

Karate-dō is a noble martial art, and the reader can rest assured that those who take pride in breaking boards or smashing tiles, or who boast of being able to perform outlandish feats like stripping flesh or plucking out ribs, really know nothing about karate. They are playing around in the leaves and branches of a great tree, without the slightest concept of the trunk.

2: ORIGINS

According to an old anecdote the Emperor Napoleon was struck with wonder and admiration upon hearing of the existence of an East Asian country which, though small, was independent and possessed no weapons. Located to the south of Japan, that country, formerly called the Kingdom of the Ryukyus and now known as Okinawa Prefecture, was the birthplace of karate.

No one knows when karate first made its appearance in our beloved Ryukyu. In the past it was always kept strictly secret from outsiders, and we have no written records to which we can turn for information.

There were two occasions in Ryukyuan history when weapons were banned by governmental edict; the first was over five centuries ago and the second, about two hundred years later. These bans cannot but have played an important role in the development of karate.

The first weapons ban was imposed during the so-called Unified Three Kingdoms period, which I believe Ba Kin mentions in his *Chinsetsu Yumihari-zuki* ("Camellia Tales of the Bow-shaped Moon"). Until the early fifteenth century the Ryukyus were split into three independent kingdoms—Chūzan, Nanzan and Hokuzan—each contending for supremacy over the others. Chūzan eventually prevailed, and the country was united under its king, the great Shō Hashi [1372–1439]. Immediately after gaining the upper hand, he set about establishing a non-military government. He issued an edict strictly prohibiting the possession of weapons, even a sword gone to rust, and called together statesmen and scholars from all over the nation to form a truly centralized administration.

For the next two centuries, the Ryukyuans enjoyed an undisturbed peace. Then in 1609, they were attacked by the Shimazu, the military governors of the Satsuma fief in southern Kyushu, who considered the southern seas part of their domain. During Japan's Sengoku [Civil War] period [1467–1568], the Shimazu forces had acquired an unequaled reputation for valor and ferocity. Only twenty-odd years prior to their attack on the Ryukyus, they had given the great Imperial Regent, Toyotomi Hideyoshi, a most difficult time in his drive to unify Japan.

The formidable Satsuma samurai met with remarkably stiff

resistance when they attacked the Ryukyus. A direct frontal assault on the port of Naha, the gateway to Okinawa, failed, and it was only after a detached force of the Shimazu army circled the island and made a surprise attack on the unguarded port of Unten that the invaders were finally able to gain a foothold. The situation then took a sudden turn for the worse, and Okinawa, the main island, soon fell into Shimazu hands.

Under the Shimazu, weapons were again banned, this time for the general populace and the upper classes alike. Most historians agree that karate, the unique Okinawan form of weaponless combat, owes its creation to this second ban, because it forced the Ryukyuans to invent a means of unarmed self-defense. However, some weaponless combat techniques must have been practiced even before the Satsuma invasion, and so it is more plausible that this new ban simply acted as a catalyst to spur the refinement of already existing techniques.

Since the Ryukyus were a tributary state of China, there had been periods of frequent contact between them and Fukien on the mainland. It would have been quite natural for Chinese kenpō [lit., "fist method"] to be imported into the islands. Elements of kenpō were probably adapted and incorporated into indigenous fighting styles. Of course, some kenpō styles may also have been passed down intact, retaining their original forms. In this manner the two precursors of karate-dō, Okinawa-te and Tō-de, were eventually born. As children, we often heard our elders speak of Tō-de and Okinawa-te, and it is quite reasonable to assume the former referred to fighting forms embodying the Chinese kenpō tradition, and the latter to native combat techniques.

The history of martial arts in China can be traced back at least six thousand years. It is said that during the reign of the mythological Yellow Emperor [Huang-ti, ca. 2700 B.C.], soldiers fought off barbarian insurgents with razor-sharp swords. From then until the reign of King Wen [Wen Wang], founder of the Chou dynasty [ca. 1027 B.C.], China was in an extremely turbulent state, marked by ongoing warfare among nomadic tribes.

During this period of strife, new stratagems and fighting techniques were constantly being invented out of a natural need to overcome enemies on the battlefield. These ancient fighting methods were systematized primarily through the efforts of three men, Ta-Shang Lao-ch'un, Ta-yi Chen-jen and Yuan Shih-t'ien, who founded what could be called the Three Primitive Schools of martial techniques. Their systems were passed down through generations of disciples, who added improvements and eventually came up with the highly refined techniques of today.

In the Three Kingdoms period [A.D. 220–80], three famous heroes, Kuan-yü, Chang Fei and Chao Yün, were able to rise in the world and perform great deeds for their countries through their prowess in martial techniques. Especially notable was Chao Yün, who, armed with only a spear, was able to drive back throngs of foes and lead his prince to safety. In succeeding periods, it became axiomatic that the commanders of large armies be men who excelled in the skills of their trade and who were very clearheaded and accomplished in strategy.

The next millenium witnessed the gradual evolution of two major styles: Shang Wu and Shaolin. Throughout the Yuan [1279–1368], Ming [1368–1644] and Ch'ing [1644–1912] dynasties, adherents of the two styles competed in polishing and perfecting them, in the process forming a number of branch schools. Needless to say, Shang Wu and Shaolin have their own particular strengths and weaknesses, and it is impossible to say which is superior. In China these arts were practiced openly, and by the end of the Ch'ing dynasty they had become widely diffused among the general population. Eventually they came to be looked upon with pride as national traditions.

The Shang Wu style founded by Chang-san Feng places primary emphasis on the power of *ch'i* (*ki* in Japanese). T'ai ch'i, Hsing-i and Pa-kua are good examples of schools exhibiting characteristics of this style. In appearance, their movements have in them an explosive power which, effectively applied, can easily knock a man down.

The Shaolin style looks upon Ta-mo Lao-tsu [Bodhidharma] as its founder. In this style, which stresses the practical application of hand and foot techniques for blocking and attacking, are seen hard-soft and long-short techniques, that is, both thrusting and short, snapping techniques.

Ta-mo is said to have journeyed to China from far-off India. After surviving the long arduous trek, crossing wide rivers, deep valleys and high mountains on the way, he arrived at the court of the Liang Emperor, to whom he preached the Buddhist Law. It was during the Cheng Kuang era [A.D. 520–4] that Ta-mo was invited by Emperor Hsiao Ming of the Northern Wei to teach at the Shaolin monastery in Honan Province.

Seeing his listeners fall unconscious from fatigue during his instruction, the great teacher told the assembled monks, "Although the teachings of the Buddhist Law are meant to nourish you spiritually, in actuality the spirit and the flesh are one. They are not intended to be separated. Looking at you now, I see you exhausted in mind and body. In your present condition, you cannot hope to complete your studies. From tomorrow, you will rise early and train in the following method." At that time he proceeded to teach the monks how to strengthen mind and body according to the *Ekikin* and *Senzui* sutras.

Senzui refers to "washing away the dust of the mind" to uncover its true light. *Ekikin*, which is composed of characters reading *eki* ["change"] and *kin* ["muscle"], means to "discipline and toughen the body." By strengthening the body through the method described in the *Ekikin* sutra, one can acquire the prowess of the Deva Kings. Polishing the mind through the *Senzui* sutra develops the strength of will to pursue a spiritual path. It is said that these two sutras together give one the power to move mountains and the ki to envelop the universe.

This method of training was the original form of training in the martial arts. The Shaolin style of kenpō eventually spread throughout China and it is still popular there today. It crossed the sea to the Ryukyus, where it probably blended with those indigenous forms it most closely resembled.

3: KARATE IN THE RYUKYUS

With weapons banned, the practice of weaponless combat methods was soon shrouded in secrecy, for the Ryukyuans were understandably reluctant to have it known that such things even existed. Fighting methods, and especially matters pertaining to karate instruction and training, were kept carefully concealed from the eyes of the Satsuma suzerains.

The practice of not revealing the principles of one's art to outsiders is not confined to karate; it is characteristic of kendo and other martial arts as well. Nevertheless, there is no comparison with the great precautions that were taken to guard karate in the Ryukyus, which included a self-imposed ban against keeping written records. In the Meiji period [1868–1912], when the need for concealment no longer existed, the centuries-old tradition of keeping karate practice and instruction secret remained deeply rooted among the people.

Since there are no written records, virtually nothing is known about those who created karate and how it was transmitted. Whatever information we have today about its historical background has been passed down by word of mouth, and precisely because of the secrecy, the oral tradition is often exasperatingly vague. Trying to sort through it for reliable facts is like trying to catch hold of clouds. As I mentioned before, even when my colleagues and I were children, everything about karate was kept strictly hidden.

Needless to say, there were no dojo as there are today and no professional instructors. The famous teacher Matsumura was a military officer serving the Ryukyuan king, and Uehara, who is said to have challenged Matsumura to a match, was a metal craftsman. Master Azato, who so kindly favored me with his special guidance and attention, was a *tonochi*, a position similar to being lord of a small fief. Master Itosu, from whom I so gratefully learned the Heian, Tekki and other kata, was the private secretary to the Ryukyuan king.

Since no one made karate his profession, the historical tradition was neglected. Those who taught karate did so only out of a personal interest, and those who studied it did so only because they liked it. When I studied under Master Azato, considered to be the greatest karate expert of his time, I was his only student; and when I trained under Master Itosu, he had very few students, fewer than even the poorest neighborhood dojo today.

The custom of secrecy lingered on in Okinawa until very recently. About ten years ago I received word from an elderly gentleman who said, "I know a kata that I have never taught to anyone but I wish to pass it on to you before I die." I deeply appreciated his kind intentions, but unfortunately I could not easily make the trip from Tokyo to Okinawa and back. For one thing, I was very busy with my work and could not take the time off. Just at that time, however, my third son Gigo had some business to attend to in Okinawa, so I asked that he be taught the kata in my place.

The old gentleman was highly elated by Gigo's arrival. When it came time to teach the kata, he securely shut all the doors and shutters so that it was impossible to peek in from the outside. When the instruction was over, the old man said, "Now I can die in peace. Among the men I refused to teach it to there was one who kept pestering me until I finally had to agree. But I altered the form and the crucial movements. So if any doubts are raised about this kata in the future, tell your father that the kata I have taught you is the correct one." When I was a youth, incidents like this were still rather commonplace.

This helps explain why there are such widely different variations in what was originally a single kata. In addition, there is always the potential problem of a student's misinterpreting a kata, thereby altering its transmission and causing distortions. But more about that later.

4: CHINESE HANDS, EMPTY HANDS

In Okinawa we always used the terms Okinawa-te and Tō-de. It was not until after I arrived in Tokyo that karate-dō began to be used by my students and myself. In *Karate-dō Kyōhan* [Tokyo: Kodansha International, 1973] I explained in detail why we employed this new term, and here I would like to again outline the reasons.

1. Since there are no written records, it is not known for sure whether the *kara* in karate was originally written with the character 唐 meaning "China" or the character 空 meaning "empty." During the time when admiration for China and things Chinese was at its height in the Ryukyus, it was the custom to use the former character when referring to things of fine quality. Influenced by this practice, in recent times karate has begun to be written with the character 唐 to give it a sense of class or elegance.

2. However, this usage can cause karate to be confused with Chinese kenpō. The kata and kumite we are now studying and our method of practice are independent of and quite different from Chinese kenpō. (Still, it should be noted that Okinawan karate today contains some kata apparently unchanged since their original transmission from China).

3. Now that Japan has become a nation of the world—some even say a nation of the first rank—it is no longer fitting to use 唐 in the name of this uniquely Japanese art.

4. *Kara* meaning "empty" implies weaponless, empty-handed self-defense, and this is appropriate.

5. Just as an empty valley can carry a resounding voice, so must the person who follows the Way of Karate make himself void or empty by ridding himself of all self-centeredness and greed. Make yourself empty within, but upright without. This is the real meaning of the "empty" in karate.

6. Once one has perceived the infinity of forms and elements in the universe, one returns to emptiness, to the void. In other words, emptiness is none other than the true form of the universe. There are various fighting techniques—*yarijutsu* ["spear techniques"] and *bōjutsu* ["stick techniques"], for example—and forms of mar-

tial arts, such as judo and kendo. All share an essential principle with karate, but karate alone explicitly states the basis of all martial arts. Form equals emptiness; emptiness equals form. The use of the character 空 in karate is indeed based on this principle.

Quite some time after I began to advocate the use of the present characters for writing karate, I received a letter of protest from a man in Okinawa. The letter said, "Recently I have heard that in Tokyo you have changed the *kara* in karate from 唐 to 空; and I wish to inquire as to your reasons for doing so. The character 唐 has been used throughout history and we are used to using it. What is one to think of its being changed so offhandedly?"

To this day there are many people in Okinawa who hold this view. In answer to the letter I could only say, "In *Karate-dō Kyōhan* I have explained my reasons in detail. I would be grateful if you would kindly refer to my explanation there."

Actually, no evidence exists linking the use of the character 唐 with the origins of karate. In olden times, people had no specific Chinese characters in mind when they spoke of karate. I myself see no point in using 唐. Furthermore, there is no more resemblance between our karate-dō and the Chinese national arts of Shaolin kenpō, Tamo-ch'uan and the like than there is between wrestling and *sumō*. Besides differences in outer appearances, there are fundamental differences in methods of training, attitude towards practice, and spirit.

In 1891 or 1892, as I recall, a certain teacher at the Shuri Jinjo Koto Shōgakkō in Okinawa began to teach karate to the students in his charge. Primary school students then were older than they are today, and students as old as twenty were not uncommon. Later, when the military draft came in, it was noted that during medical examinations those who had karate training were immediately distinguishable from the other draftees, because of their well-developed physiques, and this became a topic of conversation. As a result, the Prefectural Commissioner of Education, Ogawa Shintarō, invited Master Itosu to attend a meeting of school principals and to lead his students in a karate demonstration. Ogawa was greatly impressed by the demonstration and Itosu's opinions. Soon thereafter, in a report to the Ministry of Education, he enumerated the merits of karate. The ministry recognized the value of karate-dō training and granted permission to include karate in the physical education programs of the First Public High School of Okinawa and the Officers Candidate School.

After several centuries of being kept a closely guarded secret, karate could be taught openly for the first time. By then my colleagues and I had been involved in karate for ten years or more, but we had maintained strict silence and had not let others know.

During the Sino-Japanese War a young man trained earnestly

with Itosu for several months before joining the army. When he was assigned to the Kumamoto Division, the division medical examiner, noticing his well-balanced muscular development, said, "I hear you're from Okinawa. What martial art did you train in?" The recruit replied that farm labor was all he had ever done. But a friend who was with him blurted out, "He's been practicing karate." The doctor only murmured, "I see, I see," but he was deeply impressed.

As I will explain in the second part of this book, karate kata involve movements in all directions and so are not biased in any one direction. Furthermore, the feet are used just as much as the hands, and all types of movements, including twisting and jumping, are employed, so all four limbs are equally developed. This is one of the primary distinctive features of karate training.

One or two minutes is sufficient to complete a single kata; shorter kata require only thirty to forty seconds. Within this short duration, you train according to your own physical strength and skill. As you become more capable through practice, you are able to exert yourself more and thereby get an ample amount of exercise. To see a vigorous, robust member of a college karate club huffing and puffing after only one or two minutes of practice makes one realize how truly strenuous training can be. On the other hand, since the amount of exercise is tempered by individual skill and physical capacity, there is no danger of overexertion for the physically weak or the untrained beginner. These two aspects, the short exercise period and the fact that anyone can train regardless of build or strength, are the second distinctive feature of karate training.

Thirdly, there is no need for special equipment or facilities. Moreover, karate can be practiced alone, with another person, or with a group of a hundred or two hundred people.

If karate is used for self-defense, you can generate tremendous power that transforms your entire body into a weapon. Furthermore, in less than a year you will come to realize the resiliency of the human spirit and our great ability to polish our minds and bodies.

In May 1922, the Ministry of Education sponsored the First Annual Athletic Exhibition, which was held in Ochanomizu. As president of the Okinawan Martial Arts Association, I was asked by the Okinawan Educational Affairs Office to take advantage of this opportunity and introduce our native martial art to Japan proper. I enthusiastically agreed and started making preparations for my journey to Tokyo. Since I consider myself a poor public speaker, I wondered how to go about explaining this unique martial art to people who would be seeing and hearing of it for the first time. After much pondering, I decided to take to Tokyo with me photographs illustrating hand and foot techniques, kata and kumite; these I sorted and arranged into three scrolls.

I had originally planned to return home to Okinawa immediately after the event, but during the exhibition I received a message through Kinjō Saburō that Kanō Jigorō, the great judo master, would like to learn karate from me. Not considering myself worthy of the honor, I humbly declined, saying I would be returning home immediately after the exhibition. I offered, however, to pay a visit to his dojo before leaving. The reply was, "It would be asking too much to have you come just for me alone. Please wait two or three days. I would like everyone to see you." When I visited the Kodokan three days later, I found myself face to face with a select group of around a hundred judoka.

I had no students with me, nor even anyone to assist me. Fortunately a young man by the name of Gima Shinkin, who had been a karate instructor in Okinawa, was in Tokyo at the time attending Tokyo Shōka Daigaku (the forerunner of Hitotsubashi University). He agreed to act as my partner, and together we demonstrated kata and kumite. Several kata, notably Kankū, seemed to be especially popular with the spectators, and we were asked to perform them a number of times.

After the demonstration there were question and answer sessions, first with the younger men and then with the senior students. Later on, as we were having a pleasant chat, I was asked by Kanō Sensei how long it would take to learn all the kata. When I replied that I thought that it would take over a year, he said, "Well, I can't impose on you by asking you to stay that long, but I wish you'd teach me at least two or three." I was struck with admiration for the magnanimity of this great teacher and elder statesman of the martial arts world.

My plan to return home was put off, and beginning with the Kodokan and the Toyama Army Academy, I was soon receiving earnest requests for detailed information on karate from groups and societies as varied as the Legal Bar Association, the Secondary School Athletic Study Group, a painters' coterie called the Poplar Club, and the Shō family. Recognizing my limitations, I nevertheless felt that I should do whatever I could for the advancement of karate-dō. I did my best to visit each and every group that requested a lecture or demonstration. Gradually, the number of students taking short training courses increased, with the more serious among them becoming my disciples. Soon I was offered positions at various schools. Since then, I have been continuously engaged in these activities, and I have come to the conclusion that there is unlikely to be a chance for me to return home.

"How many styles of karate are there?" is a question I am often asked. It may seem a very simple question, but actually it is very difficult. Because karate eventually takes on a deeply personal character, it may be said that every karateka has his own karate. In fact there are simpler, less subjective factors contributing to the appearance of a wide variety of karate styles. To take one example, a person's inability to perform the correct kata movements or his failure to master techniques can lead to alterations in the kata. Or due to a lack of diligence, students may learn a form incorrectly. Other people, not having practiced for a long time, forget the original kata and make up their own movements. Some mistake their instructor's personal habits and idiosyncrasies for integral parts of the kata. We can say there are many factors that can lead to changes in a kata, but it would be a shame to consider the resulting variations as constituting truly different styles.

There are also a great many people who try to blend a little knowledge of jūjutsu with a tiny bit of karate study. The result is strange and unworthy of being called either. In the same vein, some men go about trying to sell their homemade concoctions as Such and Such Style of karate or Such and Such Style of Kenpō. It would be a great pity to call these karate styles.

Too many karate masters are that only through self-proclamation. From time to time my dojo is visited by men who announce themselves as being ''the top student of So and So Sensei.'' Unfortunately, ''top student'' can be ambiguous, and it does not necessarily follow that the person has attained a high level of skill. All too frequently these ''top students'' are extremely poor in ability. One can only wonder where the nerve to go around advertising themselves as karate experts comes from. If one takes seriously the karate of such as these, the number of styles is without limit.

A few years ago I took my students to the Butoku-den in Kyoto to participate in a dedicatory martial arts demonstration. Karate was listed in the program in the judo section. As I read through the names of the various karate groups, I was very much surprised at the great number of karate styles and schools of which I had never heard. When it came time for their demonstrations, I was even more surprised because their so-called karate was so unlike karate. Deeply embarrassed, I felt I should apologize to the other observers. It was karate that I, who have devoted many years to the art, could not recognize as such. When a student asks me how many styles of karate there are, should I mention these aberrations? Confusing the public as these men do is inexcusable.

As far as I know, the only styles that have been handed down from the past are the Gōjū-ryū of Master Miyagi and the Shito–ryu of Master Mabuni. I have never given a name to the karate I am studying, but some of my students call it *Shōtōkan-ryū.*

Looking at the kata, it is possible to roughly divide them into two general categories. The kata of the first category are heavy and hard. They are particularly suitable for building musculature and physical strength. In the second category the kata are light and quick. Agility and speed are stressed, and one can learn to move with the quickness of a falcon. Our seniors referred to the former as Shōrei-ryū and the latter as Shōrin-ryū. Rather than calling them *ryū*, "style," it may be more accurate to refer to them as *fū*, "type," "manner." At any rate, it is only a rough division, for Shōrin kata contain slow and heavy actions, and in the Shōrei kata can be seen light and quick actions. The two types of kata should be practiced and studied impartially so that one does not learn one type to the exclusion of the other.

5: MASTER AZATO

Master Azato's martial arts skill was, as I have noted, outstanding; certainly he was without equal in all of Okinawa. Happily, I was a close friend of his oldest son and had the good fortune of receiving Azato's special instruction in karate and his advice and counsel in other matters. This has always been a source of deep pride to me.

Prominent in the social structure in Okinawa were the *udon* and the *tonochi*. The *udon* comprised the lords of large fiefs and corresponded to the rank of daimyo on the Japanese mainland. The *tonochi* consisted of the hereditary chiefs of towns and villages and roughly corresponded to the mainland *shōmyō*, who were landowners on a small scale and minor lords. [For some decades after the Meiji Restoration in 1868, the place of the samurai was taken by the *shizoku* class, above whom were the former nobility and daimyo and below whom were the commoners.]

Master Azato's domain was the village of Azato, located between Naha and Shuri. He and Master Itosu were on extremely friendly terms, and it was through Azato's recommendation that Itosu was appointed the king's private secretary. Azato himself was the king's most trusted military officer, one of his functions being aide-de-camp. Since his counsel on political and administrative matters was often sought, he eventually became a kind of a privy councilor.

He would often remark to me, "Watch, Funakoshi. As soon as the Trans-Siberian Railway is completed, there'll be war between Russia and Japan." History proved him to be right, but at the time I had no idea how or why that would be so. Despite the isolation of our small island, Azato possessed penetrating insight into international affairs.

At the time of the Meiji Restoration, when the Ryukyuan kingdom had to decide which side to take [i.e., whether to remain loyal to the Tokugawa shogun or accept return to imperial rule], Azato firmly pushed for Ryukyuan support of the fledgling Meiji government. Moving with the changing times, he was also the first to cut off his long hair and topknot, long symbols of pride and manhood to the islanders. Later, as military attache and adviser to the House of Shō, he resided for many years in the Kojimachi district of Tokyo, where he was on intimate terms with many of the prominent men of the time.

I believe Azato's swordsmanship was that of the Jigen School. He seemed to have full confidence in his ability. Although he was by no means a braggart, he would sometimes smile and say jokingly, "If it comes to a life and death match with real swords, I'm sure I can handle it." That his confidence was based on real ability could be seen in a match with Master Kanna, the famous kendo expert. When Kanna attacked him straight on with an unblunted blade, Azato deflected the blade with his arm and reduced Kanna to immobility.

Kanna Yasumori was a well-known *bushi* ["warrior"]. In Okinawa, the term *bushi* did not simply refer to a man of the samurai class, but to one who was accomplished in *bushidō*, the Way of the Warrior. Master Kanna, thoroughly versed in both the Chinese and Japanese classics, was highly respected as a scholar. He was also endowed with amazing physical strength. His well-developed physique was awesome, with bull-like shoulders so prominent his neck seemed to be buried in them. People used to say, "Kanna's shoulders—two stories high," which gives some idea of his awesome appearance. Nor was he lacking in courage or fighting spirit, which were so formidable that one was reminded of a fireball surrounded by a pulsating aura.

Strange, then, that when he stood before Azato, he seemed somehow helpless. He attacked again and again, but each time Azato threw him about almost effortlessly.

Azato later told us, "Human nature can be described in terms of three basic types: full, contracting or penetrating. Kanna is of the first type—matchless in bravery and courage. Because of this, he overwhelms his opponents, seeming to almost swallow them up. In order to face this type, one must be either contracting or penetrating. As soon as Kanna faces an opponent, his mind is filled with nothing but the idea of attacking. If an opponent shows the slightest opening, Kanna arrogantly charges in, not caring whether he is being baited or not. Consequently, he is easily trapped."

Master Azato gave us many treasured words of advice that are still vividly impressed on my mind. "Think of the hands and feet of anyone who has trained in karate as swords. They can cut or kill with a touch." These words take on a deeper meaning for anyone who has actually seen Azato's karate. Once a man asked him the meaning and application of one-point fist [*ippon-ken*]. Azato rose quickly and simply said, "Come, attack me." The man attacked, punching with all his might. The master slipped the punch with an agile turn of his body, and with his one-point fist brushed the attacker's forearm downward and struck at his solar plexus. The move was so amazingly quick and perfectly executed his attacker did not even have time to blink, let alone evade the attack. Azato stopped his knuckle the thickness of a single sheet of paper away from his target. Had he not done so, the man would have been dead.

In a cold sweat, the man simply said, "I see, thank you," and withdrew. Later, when he took off his upper garment, I could see that the forearm had a deep purple bruise on it.

As far as I know, I was Master Azato's only disciple. The karate training of his oldest son he entrusted to Itosu. He once told me, "From ancient times people appreciated the difficulty of being a teacher to one's own child, and so it was a common practice to exchange children, letting others look after the education of one's children and vice versa. I will tell you many things about karate; please pass on what you learn in this way to my son." Without a doubt the greatest part of my knowledge of karate is based on the instruction that I received from him.

I was amazed at the thoroughness of his knowledge about all the martial arts experts of his time who were worthy of being called bushi. He knew the name, address, teacher, physical strength, strong and weak points of each one. He told me, "If you are attacked —no matter the time, place, or manner of attack—you should be ready to identify your assailant by knowing who lives in the area. You should already have an idea of his character, his level of skill, and in what ways he is strong and in what ways weak. Then you will have no reason to be afraid. Beyond that, you must always be knowledgeable about anyone good enough to attract attention. 'Know the enemy and know yourself: this is the secret key to strategy.'"

This advice sheds considerable light on the incident in which a youth named Kinjo Jirō, who had taken to ambushing innocent passersby, attacked Azato from behind without knowing who his intended victim was. You can easily imagine who was soundly trounced.

6: MASTER ITOSU

By a coincidence Itosu and Azato shared the same first name, Yasutsune. Physically, they were not at all alike. Master Azato was tall and broad shouldered and had fiery, piercing eyes, very readily calling to mind the bushi of old. Master Itosu was of average height, but his huge chest gave him the silhouette of a barrel. Still, his long flowing beard did not prevent his face from being as mild and genial as that of an innocent child.

Itosu's arms were amazingly strong. When drinking together, Azato and Itosu would often pass the time arm wrestling, but Azato would invariably be forced to concede defeat, even if he used both arms. Before giving in, he was apt to remark, "At times like this there's only one thing to do." He would then flick away Itosu's arm with lightning speed and thrust with a two-fingered spear hand, stopping just short of Itosu's eyes. (I should explain that Okinawan arm wrestling differs from the type seen in Tokyo. The elbows are not supported, and the contestants cross wrists with their fists clenched, the backs of the fists downward. The form is the same as that for the inside forearm block, which I will explain later).

As I mentioned earlier, I believe Itosu Sensei's proverbial grip was more a natural gift than anything acquired through training. This is illustrated by what happened one night when he was in Naha's Tsuji district. This was the area to go to for a night on the town and he was just about to enter a restaurant when a young man hidden in the shadows suddenly jumped in behind him and with a sharp kiai aimed a blow at Itosu's side. Instead of easily twisting away from the attack or turning to face his assailant, Itosu tightened his abdomen with an "Umm!" and the man's fist bounced off his body. With a cry of shocked disbelief, the attacker tried to step back, but Itosu already had a firm grip on his wrist with his right hand.

Feeling the power in Itosu's hand, the young man knew that if he struggled, his bones could easily be crushed. He could hardly breathe through the pain. Beads of sweat dripped from his forehead. Itosu, still not having turned his head, nonchalantly dragged the young man to a room at the rear of the restaurant.

Without relaxing his grip on the man's wrist, Itosu sat down and asked the startled waitress to bring food and sake. When the sake arrived, Itosu reached for a cup with his left hand and with his right hand he pulled his now trembling captive around in front of him. Finally releasing his grip, he looked at the young man's face for the first time, smiled broadly, and said, "I don't know what grudge you have against me, but why don't we have a drink?" Speechless with awe and shame, the young man bowed deeply.

Itosu's body was forged and tempered to the point of seeming invulnerable. He could take the blows of large strong men and not show any visible signs of pain or injury. Once there was a certain college karate instructor who had earned a reputation in his youth as an expert street fighter. To test his skills, he made a habit of waiting along the roadside to challenge passersby and provoke them into fights. Until one day his hot-blooded impetuosity allowed a very foolish idea to enter his head: "Everyone talks about what a great expert old Itosu Sensei is. But so what? If I can catch him off guard and attack from behind, he doesn't stand a chance!"

He then began looking for an opportunity. One night he thought his chance had come when he spied Itosu returning from a party. Waiting until Itosu had passed by, he stealthily slipped in behind him and without a word thrust at a vital point on the master's back. As you might expect, Itosu casually walked on without ever looking back or missing a step. The attacker's momentum carried his fist to the master's side. Itosu grabbed the wrist and tucked it neatly under his arm. Seized in this viselike grip capable of crushing green bamboo stalks, the man's arm went numb. He used his free hand to strike at his captor repeatedly, but Itosu paid not the slightest attention.

The college instructor finally cried out in desperation, "M-M-Master, forgive me, please!"

Master Itosu walked on. After a while, in a calm tranquil voice he asked, "Who are you, anyway?"

"My name is Saburō," came the reply.

For the first time Itosu turned to look. "So, you're Saburō, eh?" Then laughing he added, "Saburō, you shouldn't play mean tricks on old men."

With that he released his captive's arm. This was very typical of Master Itosu.

The author's son, Gigo Funakoshi, demonstrates Morote Kakiwake-uke

Master Funakoshi's calligraphy: *Hatsuun Jindō*
(Parting the clouds. Seeking the way.)

1953 Master Funakoshi (center)

1954 Master Funakoshi (center) at a Karate meet at Chuo University

The traditional method of demonstrating the power of the punch by breaking boards or tiles. Many schools have now dropped this practice.

Demonstrating the kick.

Kumite (sparring) demonstrated by Shigeru
Egami (left) and Gigo Funakoshi: Age-uke (top),
Gyaku-zuki (bottom)

Kumite demonstrated by Shigeru Egami (left)
and Gigo Funakoshi: Oi-zuki (top), Haito
Uchi (middle), Kentsui Uchi (bottom)

Gigo Funakoshi demonstrates Uraken Uchi

Gigo Funakoshi demonstrates Jōdan Keage

Jōdan Yoko Keage

7: TRAINING PRECEPTS

Before explaining the technical aspects of karate, I would like to give the reader general instructions on how to approach practice, and to say something about the attitudes one should have toward karate training.

First, since karate is a martial art, you must practice with the utmost seriousness from the very beginning. This means going beyond being simply diligent or sincere in your training. In every step, in every movement of your hand, you must imagine yourself facing an opponent with a drawn sword.

Each and every punch must be made with the power of your entire body behind it, with the feeling of destroying your opponent with a single blow. You must believe that if your punch fails, you will forfeit your own life. Thinking this, your mind and energy will be concentrated, and your spirit will express itself to the fullest. No matter how much time you devote to practice, no matter how many months and years pass, if your practice consists of no more than moving your arms and legs, you might as well be studying dance. You will never come to know the true meaning of karate.

You will find that training with a deadly serious attitude will over time benefit not only your study of karate, but many other facets of life as well. Life itself is often akin to a match with real swords. With a lukewarm attitude toward life—such as assuming that after every failure you will always have a second chance—what can you hope to accomplish in a short life span of fifty years?

Secondly, try to do exactly as you are taught without complaining or quibbling. Only those lacking in zeal and unwilling to face up to themselves resort to quibbling. Often their foolish complaints border on the pathetic. For example, in teaching the back stance, I come across people who say they simply are not able to learn the stance, no matter how hard they try. They ask me what they should do—after practicing for less than an hour! Even if one fervently practices the back stance every day, standing until his legs become as hard as rock, it would still require six months to a year to learn it. It is ridiculous to say, "No matter how hard I try," without first working up a sweat. A Zen monk hearing this would probably shout and scold and give the man a taste of his staff.

You cannot train through words. You must learn through your body. Enduring pain and anguish as you strive to discipline and polish yourself, you must believe that if others can do it, you can do it too. Ask yourself, "What's stopping me? What am I doing wrong? Is something lacking in my approach?" This is training in the martial arts.

Important points taught us by others may quickly be forgotten, but the essence of the knowledge acquired through personal hardship and suffering will never be forgotten. I believe that is why the martial arts masters of old would confer a diploma and reveal key elements only to those disciples whose training, almost unbearably hard and austere, had lead them to experience directly the spirit of budō.

Thirdly, when you are learning a new technique, practice it wholeheartedly until you truly understand it. Do not crave to know everything all at once. Practice painstakingly. Karate has many techniques and kata. Do not fall into the trap of thinking that because there is so much to learn, you should quickly learn everything in a general way. It would be quite impossible for an inexperienced person not knowing the meanings of the kata or the techniques contained in them to commit them all to memory. To him the kata would be nothing but an incoherent jumble of techniques. Learning each movement and each technique independently, he would fail to see how kata interrelate with kata and how kata integrate movements and techniques. Learning one thing, forgetting another, his final reward would be total confusion.

A student well versed in even one technique will naturally see corresponding points in other techniques. An upper level punch, a lower level punch, a front punch and a reverse punch are all essentially the same. Looking over the thirty-odd kata, he should be able to see that they are essentially variations on just a handful. If you truly understand a single technique, you need only observe the forms and be told the essential points of the others. You will be able to grasp them in a relatively short time.

There is the following story about a certain Gidayū master. While still a student intent on learning to chant these long narrative tales, he had an extremely strict teacher, who for many years refused to teach him more than a certain single passage from the *Taikōki*, a drama about the life and times of Toyotomi Hideyoshi. Hundreds of times a day, day after day, the student was made to intone the same passage, and each time his teacher's sole remark was, "Not quite." He would not allow him to proceed to the next passage.

Finally, the exasperated student decided he was not suited to the profession and ran away in the dead of night to try his hand at something more congenial in the shogun's capital of Edo. On the way, he happened to stop for the night at an inn in Suruga Province [now Shizuoka Prefecture], where a group of Gidayū enthusiasts had gathered for an amateur contest. Still deeply attached to an art in which he had long trained, the man could not resist the urge to join in. Though an outsider, he took the stage and with all his heart recited the only passage he knew well. When he had finished, he was approached by the old man who had sponsored the contest. "My, that was truly splendid," remarked the old man. "I'd like to know your real name. Unless my eyes and ears deceive me, you must be a famous master."

The erstwhile student was at a loss to respond to such flattering praise. Scratching his head, he blurted out, "Nothing could be farther from the truth. I'm just a rank amateur. I have to admit I don't even know the passages before or after the one I just recited."

The old man was greatly surprised. "Is that true? But your skill ranks with the Bunraku masters. Who on earth was your teacher?"

The student told about the severity of his training and how he had finally given up and run away.

With a sigh the old man said, "You've made a terrible mistake. It is precisely because you were blessed by such a strict teacher that you have learned so much in only a few years. Take my advice: go back to your teacher immediately, ask his forgiveness, and resume your study."

Hearing the old man's appraisal, the student suddenly realized his error and went back to his teacher. Eventually he came to be a master of his art. I think this story is about none other than Master Koshiji, but whoever it was, it raises a number of points worth pondering.

Fourthly, don't pretend to be a great master and don't try to show off your strength. It is absurd that many of those practicing the martial arts feel they must make a show of being a martial artist. Picture a man, shoulders raised high, elbows swinging, swaggering down the street as if he owned it, with a look on his face that says, "I'm the greatest hero that ever lived." Even if he were that, one's respect for him would drop by at least half. And, of course, if he was not a man of great ability but simply a synthetic hero, the situation would be too ridiculous for words.

The tendency to act big or superior is usually most conspicuous among novices. By acting this way, they degrade and ruin the reputation of those seriously practicing martial arts. Then there are those who, having a superficial knowledge of one or two karate techniques, hold their fists in such a way as to call attention to their calloused knuckles while pushing their way through crowds as if looking for a fight—foolish beyond words.

"His smile can win even the hearts of little children; his anger can make a tiger crouch in fear." This succinctly describes the true martial artist.

A fifth point to remember is that you must always have a deep regard for courtesy, and you must be respectful and obedient toward your seniors. There is no martial art that does not stress the importance of courtesy and respectful manners.

Courtesy and respect should not be confined to the dojo. Is there anyone who would bow before the shrine in the dojo but walk right past a wayside shrine without paying his respects? I would hope not. Similarly, is there anyone who willingly follows the orders of his seniors in the dojo but completely ignores the words of his father and older brother? I hope not. If there is such a person, he has no right to practice a martial art.

At home one listens to one's father and older brothers. In school one obeys one's teachers and upper classmen. In the army one follows the orders of officers and non-coms. At work one does not act contrary to or disregard the words of superiors. Because of this, there is value in one's having practiced karate.

Sixthly, you must ignore the bad and adopt the good. When you observe the practice of others and discover something that you should learn, try to master it without hesitation. If you see a man sliding into idleness, examine yourself with strict eyes. When you see a man who is particularly good at kicking, ask yourself why his kick is so good. How can you learn to kick like that; how does your kick differ? In this manner, you should be able to devise a method to improve your kick. When you see a man who does not seem to improve, again ask yourself why. Maybe he does not train enough or maybe he lacks determination. Ask yourself, does not the same hold true for you?

This attitude does not apply only to improving one's technical abilities. We all have our good points and our shortcomings. If we are sincere in our desire to improve ourselves, everyone we meet can be a role model and a touchstone for self-reflection. An old proverb says, *Sannin okonaeba kanarazu waga shi ari.* [This is based on a passage from the *Analects* of Confucius: "When I walk along with two others, they may serve me as my teachers. I will select their good qualities and follow them, their bad qualities and avoid them."]*

Seventh, think of everyday life as karate training. Do not think of karate as belonging only to the dojo, nor only as a fighting method. The spirit of karate practice and the elements of training are applicable to each and every aspect of our daily lives. The spirit born of bearing down and gritting your teeth against the cold in winter training or blinking the sweat out of your eyes in summer training can serve you well in your work. And the body that has been forged in the kicks and blows of intense practice will not succumb to the trials of studying for a difficult exam or finishing an irksome task. One whose spirit and mental strength have been strengthened by sparring with a never-say-die attitude should find no challenge too great to handle. One who has undergone long years of physical pain and mental agony to learn one punch, one kick should be able to face any task, no matter how difficult, and carry it through to the end. A person like this can truly be said to have learned karate.

*The Chinese Classics, Vol. I: Confucian Analects, The Great Learning, The Doctrine of the Mean. trans. James Legge. Hong Kong: Hong Kong University Press, 1960.

8: BEFORE PRACTICE

As Master Azato's warning to "regard your opponent's hands and feet as swords" indicates, practically every part of the body, from the top of one's head to the tips of one's toes, has a potential as some sort of weapon.

The hand alone can be given more than ten different forms for striking, each form making use of a particular area of the hand. The main forms are: *seiken*, "regular fist"; *uraken*, "back fist"; *shuken*, "hand fist"; *ippon-ken*, "single-point index-finger fist"; *chūkōken/nakadakaken*, "single-point middle-finger fist"; *tettsui*, "iron hammer"; *nukite*, "spear hand"; *nihon nukite*, "two-finger spear hand"; *ippon nukite*, "one-finger spear hand"; *shutō*, "sword hand"; and *haishu*, "back of the hand."

Forms of the foot from the ankle down include: *koshi*, "ball of the foot"; *sokutō*, "sword foot"; *tsumasaki*, "toe tips"; *enshō*, "back of the heel"; and *sokkō*, "top of the foot."

The wrists, elbows, knees, and so on are commonly used, so it is indeed no exaggeration to say the entire body is a weapon.

Power and strength in karate are dependent on constantly training and polishing oneself in the use of various parts of the body. It goes without saying that one's techniques are only as good as they are reliable in time of need.

Be careful not to be like those who do not train sufficiently yet become "masters" because their talk resembles that of the experts. From olden times these men have been called *kuchi bushi*, a derogatory term written with characters meaning *kuchi*, "mouth," and *bushi*, "warrior." Even today, these "mouth warriors" are as common as grains of sand on a beach.

One begins to practice karate by learning how to make a proper fist. Then one is taught the basic stances, postures, blocks and attacks and repeats them over and over again.

Thrusting one's fist out in a punch may seem extremely elementary—even for a child. Yet to develop a flawless punch is far from easy. It takes a great deal of effort, endurance and resourcefulness over a number of years to learn how to punch correctly. It is not hard to simply memorize the movements and techniques of karate, but karate is not something to be learned superficially or grasped with the intellect alone. Karate demands to be forged and polished. I sincerely hope that you fully understand this.

After one has a general understanding of the basic techniques, one learns kata. In this book, I have explained the Ten no Kata. These kata, which were developed at the Shōtōkan, are composed of basic blocking and attacking techniques that are simple for beginners to learn.

The various kata were created by masters and experts of the past whose names are largely unknown. The methods of attack and defense that they used in creating these kata were born, forged and tested through personal experience.

As I mentioned earlier, originally there were no written records relating to karate, so perpetuation of a kata depended entirely on the personal recollections and skills of those who practiced it. It is only reasonable to assume that lapses in memory or misunderstanding of kata would have contributed to errors in transmission. Without records it is impossible to verify anything. The only means we have at our disposal to evaluate the kata that are doubtful, or the ones that need to be researched more thoroughly, is to become adept at them through practice piled on practice. Then, based on the accumulated experience, we can finally arrive at a personal evaluation or opinion.

At the Shōtōkan we are presently studying and investigating the following kata: Ten no Kata, Chi no Kata, Hito no Kata, Heian Shodan, Heian Nidan, Heian Sandan, Heian Yodan, Heian Godan, Tekki Shodan, Tekki Nidan, Tekki Sandan, Bassai Dai, Bassai Sho, Kankū Dai, Kankū Sho, Empi, Gankaku, Jutte, Hangetsu, Jion, Meikyō, Hakkō, Kiun, Shōtō, Shōin, Hotaku and Shōkyō.

As I mentioned before, in studying kata the most important thing is to concentrate on learning each thoroughly. There is infinitely greater value in studying a single kata until one has digested it well than in possessing a shallow knowledge of thirty kata.

After you have come to understand the meanings of the arm and leg movements and the essential elements of attack and defense contained in the kata, you can start to practice *kumite*, "sparring." The practice of basic techniques and kata can be done alone, but kumite requires a partner. In kumite practice you take the techniques learned in kata and apply them realistically, with one person attacking and the other concentrating on blocking and counterattacking. Through kumite you will come to appreciate the difficulty of striking a moving target or blocking an unexpectedly swift attack. You will be made aware of the vital importance of speed in footwork and in twisting the hips, of correct breathing, of maai and so on. You will study methods of feinting and penetrating your opponent's defenses, and you will recognize how essential a vigorous and heroic feeling and a strong fighting spirit are. Lastly, you will come to a deep realization that beyond what we think of as the best, there is always something better.

During this time you must never cease to painstakingly pursue the study of basics, specifically, punching, kicking and blocking. Besides mastering all the blocks and attacks in the kata, you must also investigate and devise techniques appropriate to your own age, build, height and individual characteristics.

For example, a man over 180 centimeters tall will not be attacked very often in the face, but he will frequently encounter attacks to his chest or below the belt. Accordingly, he should study middle and lower level blocks with particular care. Similarly, a short or weak person would fail miserably if he chose techniques dependent on physical power. Instead he should take advantage of quick movements, or give more than usual attention to ways of getting inside his opponent's defenses. If you study carelessly or haphazardly, your kata and techniques will never come to life. It is important that you always try to discover and practice the techniques most suitable to your own situation.

9: FIST AND FOOT

In this chapter I would like to explain in general about the two parts of the body most frequently employed in karate, the fist and the foot.

There are various ways of making a fist. Among them, the most basic of all is the *seiken*, "regular fist." Learning to make *seiken* correctly is of the utmost importance, so you should follow the illustrations closely. A fist improperly made cannot be strong and is liable to cause needless injury to the hand.

First, fold the tips of the fingers tightly (fig. 1) and curl them deeply into the palm of the hand (fig. 2). Fold the thumb over, pressing it lightly against the index and middle fingers (fig. 3). Note in the profile view of the fist in figure 4 how the fist is clenched so tightly the knuckles tend to form an acute rather than a right angle. Of course, not many people will be able to make such a tight fist in the beginning, and after clenching their fists for one or two minutes, their arms will probably become tired. With continued practice you will be able to fold your fingers deeply into a tight fist, and your knuckles will develop to the point where they will form a right angle.

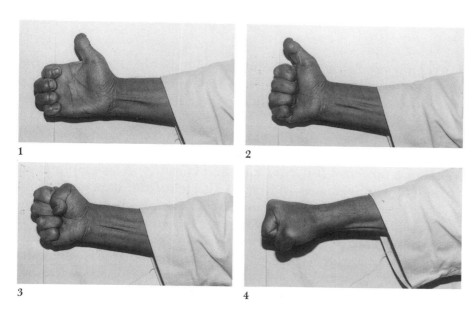

1

2

3

4

At first glance, it may seem that the exposed thumb is in danger, but such is not the case. Forming the fist in this way is a tried and true method based on long years of experience in karate-dō. In fact, tucking the thumb inside the fingers creates a much greater risk of its being damaged while striking. In any case, injuries are more frequent if the fist is loose or the fingers slack.

It is practically certain that eight or nine out of ten beginners will make a fist with their wrist slightly bent so that the back of the fist meets the wrist at an upward oblique angle (fig. 5). If you punch with your wrist like this, you make contact with the middle joints of the fingers rather than with the knuckles where the fingers join the hands, thus running the risks of injuring the fingers or spraining the wrist. Similarly, if the wrist is bent downward as in figure 6, there is a danger of spraining it. The fist must be thrust straight out, as in thrusting with a spear. When practicing, always be careful that your fist does not wander to the right, left, up or down.

5

6

When your fist strikes the target you should not let even the slightest bit of force escape; the power of the punch should flow in a direct line through the arm and converge in the knuckles of the index and middle fingers.

The seiken is truly the life of karate-dō, and the karateka cannot neglect the constant training of his fists, not even for a day. Without a powerful fist, your kata and kumite will lack authenticity and your movements will be no different from dancing.

To a certain extent, basics and kata are helpful in strengthening your fists. But in either case, you are only punching air so there is no resistance or response, and never having had a chance to test it, you cannot really have confidence in your punch. This is where the *makiwara* [*lit.* "sheared straw"; here the padded rice-straw striking post] plays an important role.

In karate-dō, the makiwara is used to strengthen not only the fist, but to practice use of the sword hand, elbows and feet. The explosive power behind the karate strikes and kicks can be attributed to training with the makiwara.

The best material for the striking post is Japanese cypress, because it is resilient, strong and resistant to the elements; however, cedar can be used as a substitute. The post should be about 2.1 meters long and 9 centimeters wide. It should be 9 centimeters thick at the bottom, tapering to about 1.6 centimeters at the top. (It is a good idea to simply take a length of post 9 centimeters square and saw it diagonally lengthwise to obtain two posts.) At least one-third of the post must be buried in the ground, but the height at which you fix the straw pad will depend on your own height. Ideally, the top of the post should come to chest level; in most cases, leaving approximately 1.2 meters of the post exposed should suffice. Wet the earth around the base of the post and pack it firmly to keep the post from falling backward under repeated blows.

The pad itself is made by tightly wrapping braided straw around a straw core. When finished, the striking surface should be softened with a mallet. Even then, beginners may not be able to hit it without experiencing pain, so you may want to wrap it with a towel or an old cloth. If you overdo it even slightly you'll break the skin on your knuckles.

Remember that moisture is the worst enemy of the straw, causing it to rot easily. The straw pad should be covered completely when not in use to protect it. An empty oil can or a discarded bucket will do just fine.

Having made a makiwara, you can begin strengthening your fists. Extend your arm and take a position in front of it so that you can reach it comfortably. Stand in a *hanmi*, "half-facing," posture, bending your knees deeply and dropping your hips as low as possible. Hold your front hand in a fist about 13 or 15 centimeters above your front knee. Position your other hand at your waist with the back of your hand facing downward. Keep your chin in and look straight ahead at the makiwara. Lower your shoulders and put power in the lower abdomen. Refer to figure 7 and pay especially close attention to your lower legs and feet. The feet should be planted firmly, almost as if rooted in the ground. This is the basic ready position for using the striking post. (For more detailed explanations, refer to the sections on *zenkutsu-dachi*, "front stance" and *fudō-dachi*, "immovable stance." Note that if the straw pad is too high, your legs will naturally straighten to some extent, causing the hips to rise and allowing power to escape. Actually, it is preferable to position the pad so that it feels as if it is almost a little too low.

7   8

With a feeling of striking with your shoulder, rotate your hips
and thrust punch with the fist that had been held at your hip (fig. 8).
Put your whole body behind the punch while simultaneously pulling your other hand to your hip. As you punch, rotate the striking
fist so that the back of the fist faces upward, and hit the target as if
screwing your fist into it. The pulling hand should be rotated so
that the back of the fist is downward by the time it reaches your
hip. This fist rotation is rather difficult for beginners at first, so you
should practice it a little before actually hitting the makiwara.

Since the post is thinner at the top than at the bottom, it will
tend to spring back when struck hard. Thrust deeply and solidly to
minimize this tendency.

If you are right-handed, you should practice more with your left
hand than your right (and vice versa) to prevent bias in your techniques. As a general rule, the more punches the better, but in the
beginning, when your fists are not yet toughened, I recommend
not using full power. Gradually, as your fists become stronger,
you should shift your emphasis from quantity to quality. Put all
your strength into each punch while trying to grasp the main points
of the thrust punch: keep your stance low, rotate your hips, and
concentrate the power of your entire body into your fist. Just using
the post to raise blood blisters on the knuckles is foolish; even more
foolish is feeling self-satisfied with your blisters.

Besides broken skin and pain, there is the problem of missing the
center of the target, since you are twisting your hips and punching
with all your might at an object 90 centimeters away from you.
When your fist does not hit dead center, it has a tendency to slide,
and when it does so, even slightly, there's a second cause for
scraped knuckles. Swollen fists can be soaked in cold water to ease
the pain and make the swelling subside, but if you break the skin,
you won't be able to use the makiwara for a week or two. There
are, of course, those stout-hearted high school and college students
who, hating to lose, ignore abraded skin, grit their teeth, and go on

striking the straw pad until it is dyed deep red with their blood. Their spirit is admirable, but they can't help throwing weaker and weaker punches. In the end there is not much benefit.

I would now like to discuss a few other important hand techniques:

Uraken. The fist is formed in the same way as seiken, but as the name indicates, the back of the fist is employed. The striking area is mainly the base of the knuckles of the index and middle fingers (fig. 9). When training with the makiwara, contact is made with almost the entire back surface of the hand. Executed correctly, a back fist strike is very powerful. It is mainly used against the face, armpits, ribs below the arms and so on. It is very effective against an opponent who attacks from the side or who pivots to the side after an initial frontal attack.

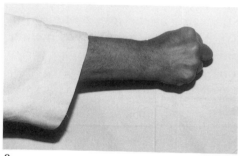

9

Tettsui. The fist is the same as the seiken, but the striking surface is the cushion on the little finger side (the area used by a masseur to pound shoulders). The obvious question is, if the iron hammer is used to massage stiff shoulders, how can it be effective as an attack? But a tettsui strike honed through practice on the makiwara can deliver remarkable force. Since the striking area is fleshy and resilient, one can hit objects quite forcefully without fear of injury. The iron hammer can be used to hit and sweep away an opponent's wrist and is an excellent weapon for attacking joints.

Nukite. As the name implies, the spear hand is used to figuratively pierce one's opponent with the fingertips. In addition to the *nukite* with the fingers held together (also called *shihon nukite*, "four-finger spear hand"), there are *nihon nukite*, "two-finger spear hand," and *ippon nukite*, "one-finger spear hand." In *shihon nukite* the fingers are held together fully extended, with the thumb retracted and folded tightly (fig. 10). Since one is thrusting hard with the fingertips, it may seem that any injury would be to one's own fingers rather than the opponent. However, this technique can be used with great effect in attacking the face or the pit of the stomach. The danger lies in the fingers being bent back and sprained or dislocated. It is best, therefore, to have the feeling of slightly folding them inward. [It should be noted that this is more of a sensation than a visibly verifiable fact.]

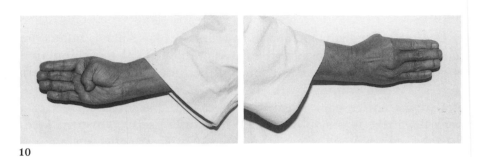

10

Shutō. The sword hand has a wide variety of applications. The hand is formed exactly like the four-finger spear hand, but the striking area is the side of the palm, the same as the iron hammer but with the fingers extended (fig. 10). The many target areas include the ribs, arms and legs. The name shutō obviously implies use of the hand as a sword, and so one attacks the neck or arms as though to cut them off. After the seiken, the sword hand is the most important attack weapon. Through practice on the makiwara, one's shutō can come to pack a terrific amount of force.

Enpi. The elbow is used with extreme effectiveness in karate. It can be used to either attack or block. The elbow is very sturdily made, and if she knows how to use it skillfully, even a woman or a girl can easily knock down a large opponent. From ancient times, the riposte most feared by men has been the female elbow. The elbow can be used in many ways: striking an opponent who comes to seize you from the rear (*ushiro enpi*), against an attack from the side (*yoko enpi*), striking an opponent who has ducked and is attacking from a low position (*shita enpi*), or striking an opponent as you pull him toward you (*mawashi enpi*). Among target areas are the face, chest, ribs, head, back—almost anywhere. Defensively, it can be used to protect the chest and sides. An elbow strike to the back of an attacker's fist or the top of his foot is in most cases sufficient to make him change his mind and break off his attack.

Feet and Legs

Now I would like to explain a little more about foot techniques. The role played by feet in karate is so conspicuous as to make it one of karate's distinguishing features. They are mainly used for kicking, but there are leg blocks and leg sweeps. The legs are, of course, thicker and stronger than the arms, but at the same time much more difficult to learn to use effectively. Obviously, whenever one leg is raised from the ground, the other must support the entire body. A clumsy kick can destroy one's balance, or if slow, the kicking leg can be seized by the opponent. In any case, a poorly executed kick can leave one extremely vulnerable. On the other hand, a well-practiced kick can take an opponent by surprise and be virtually unblockable.

Koshi. The ball of the foot also goes by the rather exotic sounding name, "tiger's paw." We might also draw attention to the fact that the front of the foot takes on the shape of a pigeon's breast when the toes are raised back strongly (fig. 11). This part of the foot, used for kicking to the front, is the most fundamental of all kicking weapons, occupying the same position of importance that the seiken does among hand techniques. One should be careful to bend the toes back sufficiently and to put strength into the ankle when kicking. Failure to do so will result in injury.

Enshō. As indicated in figure 11, this refers specifically to the back of the heel. Used mainly for kicking to the rear, it can be applied when one's arms are twisted behind one's back, or when one is suddenly attacked from behind.

Tsumasaki. Used in kicking to the front, the toe tips are extended straight out, or with the second toe crossed over the big toe (fig. 12). At first there is a danger of spraining one's toes, but with sufficient practice, the risk of injury is diminished. Toe tips can be extremely effective when directed at the pit of the stomach or the lower abdomen.

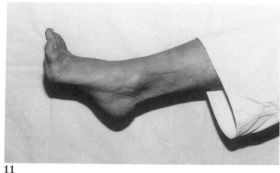

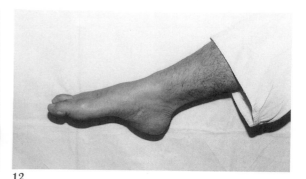

11

12

Sokutō. The toes are raised as in the *koshi*, but the striking surface of the sword foot is the outside edge of the foot, close to the heel (fig. 13). Used in kicking to the side, stamping and so on, it may well be a weapon unique to karate. The target areas include the ribs and knees and since it usually comes as a surprise to those who do not know karate, it can be quite effective.

Sokutei. The sole of the foot can be employed as in judo to sweep the opponent's foot out from under him. With practice it can be used to sweep away his fist.

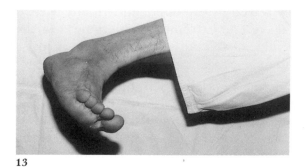

13

10: STANCE

Let's talk about stances. You may think that any human being at least knows how to stand, but in karate, we have stances such as *kutsu-dachi*, ''back stance''; *fudō-dachi*, ''immovable stance''; and *kiba dachi*, ''straddle leg stance'' that are extremely difficult to master, even after years of practice. In fact, stance is so important in karate that just by looking at a man's stance, one can tell his level of ability. Realizing that no matter how detailed my explanation is, words alone cannot teach you how to stand correctly, I have decided to give here only the key points about the various stances.

Heisoku-dachi, ''feet together stance.'' In this stance, the big toes of both feet are brought together, pointing straight ahead. You can think of this as standing at attention.

Musubi-dachi, ''informal attention stance, toes out.'' This stance is basically like that of standing at attention, but with the toes apart, the feet form a V. There are some important differences, too. In karate, you must be prepared to react immediately to a change in any situation. This latitude of response is not possible if you are standing rigidly, as you would be at attention. Do not puff out your chest unnecessarily or lock the knees. Lower your shoulders and breathe from the lower abdomen. Your posture should be as natural as possible.

Hachinoji-dachi, ''open leg stance.'' This resembles musubi-dachi, but heels are about 30 centimeters apart. The character *hachi* of *hachinoji* means ''eight'' and the position of the feet in this stance resembles the character. The key points here are the same as those for musubi-dachi. This stance is frequently seen at the beginning and end of kata.

Zenkutsu-dachi (or simply *zenkutsu*), ''front stance.'' In this stance the feet are separated with the front leg bent and the back leg extended (fig. 1). The distance between the feet depends on one's height, but the average is about 75 centimeters. Beginners should make the distance a little longer. The shin of the front leg should be perpendicular to the floor with the knee bent as much as possible to lower the hips. Take care that the heel of the back leg does not rise off the floor and make sure both feet point in the same direction. The upper torso should be upright, with strength concentrated in the lower abdomen. The weight of the entire body must be squarely above the legs. In karate, advancing movements are generally executed using *zenkutsu-dachi*, but since beginners tend to place too much weight on the front leg, when practicing they should put 60 percent of their power in the back leg. When the right foot is forward, the stance is called a *migi zenkutsu*, "right front stance," and when the left foot is forward, it is *hidari*, "left," *zenkutsu*.

Kōkutsu-dachi, "back stance." This stance is generally considered to be the opposite of the front because the back leg is bent. It is a very hard stance to master. The back leg must be bent as much as possible while supporting the full weight of the body. The front leg is bent only slightly, with the toe tips just barely touching the floor. Because it is so difficult to carry the whole body, the back leg usually does not bend sufficiently. As a result, the center of gravity tends to rise, and the upper torso is apt to lean forward. The feet should be positioned so that their axis forms a right angle. Figure 2 should be studied carefully.

Fudōdachi, "immovable stance." In this stance, the legs are separated slightly more than in the back stance, with both knees fully bent and body weight equally distributed. Both feet should point in the same direction.

Kiba-dachi, "straddle leg stance." In this stance, the feet are spread to the left and right with the toes pointing just slightly inward (fig. 3). The knees are fully bent and opened so that the legs from the knees down are nearly perpendicular to the ground. The soles of the feet must be in complete contact with the floor, as if

1 2

clinging tight, but the toes should rest lightly. The upper torso should be erect, and power concentrated in the lower abdomen. This is also an extremely difficult stance and is not easy to understand even after one or two years of hard practice. "Horse riding," the meaning of *kiba* and the alternative name of the stance, derives from the fact that the position of the legs resembles a person on horseback. This is the best stance for training and strengthening the legs.

3

11: TEN NO KATA

Ten no kata, as I have already indicated, is not a kata handed down from the past. Rather, it is composed of movements I have selected from the thirty-odd traditional kata that form the nucleus of karate-dō. My primary basis for selection was the suitability of the movements for beginners. This kata can be practiced alone, but it is especially appropriate for group training.

The principal consideration was to design a kata that can be learned readily by anyone. Prior experience in the martial arts is unnecessary, and this kata can be performed by women, children, the elderly—just about anyone who is able to do simple calisthenics. It can be performed anywhere there is room enough to take a step forward—in a garage, corridor, veranda, even your living room.

Only about two minutes is required to perform the kata, so no matter how busy you are, you can take time to practice this kata once, or if time allows, more than once.

No special clothing is needed. Since freedom of movement is necessary, athletic wear is best but you can practice while wearing an ordinary shirt and trousers or the casual clothes you wear around the house.

If you are ready to begin—actually, since you need no special place, time or equipment, the only preparation being a desire to learn the kata—why don't we start right now? There are just two or three points I would like to mention before explaining the movements of the kata.

Ten no Kata is composed of two parts: *Omote*, "front," and *Ura*, "back." *Omote* consists of ten movements and is meant to be performed without a partner. The basic elements of all the kata in karate-dō are contained in this *Omote*. *Ura* consists of six movements and, being a form of kumite, it must be practiced with a partner. In *Ura*, one person attacks with a punch while his partner tries to apply the blocks and counterattacks practiced in *Omote*.

The first four movements in Omote are basic punches. (Since no blocking is involved, these are not included in *Ura*.) The next three movements (E through G) are blocks against lower level (below the belt) and middle level (between neck and belt) attacks, with a counterattack accompanying the block. The last three movements (H through J) are practiced against upper level (face) attacks.

There are two kinds of basic thrust punches: *oi-zuki* [*lit.* "pursuing punch" but more commonly lunge punch, front punch or straight punch], and *gyaku-zuki*, "reverse punch." In *oi-zuki*, the right leg advances and the punch is made with the right fist. In *gyaku-zuki*, if the right leg is brought forward, the punch is made with the left fist. In other words, the fist and leg are "reversed," which is what *gyaku* means.

The four stances in Ten no Kata are *hachinoji-dachi*, *kōkutsu-dachi*, *zenkutsu-dachi* and *fudō-dachi*. These have already been described in the chapter on stances.

In the beginning, block and counterattack should be executed as two separate techniques. This is to ensure that the block is complete and the counter strong and precise. Later, the block and counter must become as one, that is, at the instant you block, you should already be countering with gyaku-zuki. If there is the slightest lapse of time between block and counter, the attacker can recover from the block and launch a second attack. It is vital, therefore, that you become proficient in carrying out block and counterattack as one continuous action.

Normally, each movement is performed twice—first left, then right—but of course you are free to increase or decrease the number of repetitions according to the time available.

Your entire energy should be concentrated at the instant of blocking and attacking. Each technique must be accompanied by a vigorous kiai that is generated from the lower abdomen and fills your whole being with spirit. Martial arts without kiai are like a person devoid of a soul.

Ideally you should be prepared to block even an opponent who attacks as though he were breaking through a wall of steel. In counterattacking such a spirited opponent, if you do not let go with a kiai at the instant of striking, your fist will bounce off him ineffectually, your blocks will be inadequate, your punches impotent— not martial arts at all and consequently certainly not karate.

TEN NO KATA OMOTE

A. MIDDLE LEVEL THRUST PUNCH *Chūdan Oi-zuki*

Begin by taking the feet together stance and bowing respectfully. At the command of *Yōi*, "Ready," take a natural stance by opening the feet, moving the left foot outward first and then the right. Hold the fists lightly extended in front of the thighs (figs. 1–2). Lower the shoulders, look straight ahead, settle and concentrate power in the lower abdomen.

1   2

1. From a yōi posture, take a large step forward with the right leg into the right front stance while pulling the left fist back (back of the fist downward, little finger lightly touching the left side) and thrusting the right fist forward (at the level of your solar plexus) into a *chūdan*, "middle level," attack (figs. 3–4). At the moment of *kimete*, "focus," let go with a vigorous kiai.

Since the right fist is withdrawn to the hip before being thrust forward, the key points about punching the makiwara should be studied thoroughly. The hips should twist sharply. The upper body should not lean forward. The right shoulder should not extend in front of the body; both shoulders should be low and the underarm muscles tightened. The front leg should not be overly tense. At the instant of punching, power should be concentrated in the lower abdomen.

With so many points to keep in mind, the beginner is apt to be totally confused. It goes without saying that the student will not be able to satisfy all these conditions from the start. As a first step, it is sufficient to simply learn the correct order of the kata—and to not confuse right and left! Lack of synchronization of the punching hand and the pulling hand and the hands and legs is permissible at this stage. With repeated practice, they will start to move together, and the movements will be smooth and well managed. Then is the time to conform to each of the above conditions one at a time. Expecting to execute the movements skillfully from the start is evidence of false pride and overconfidence. It is more important to recognize our faults and to improve ourselves step by step.

2. Bring the right leg back to the starting position while lowering the fists, thus returning to the yōi posture (fig. 5).

This movement should be performed deliberately and without hurry. *Without hurry* does not mean *leisurely*. On the contrary, you must be fully aware and prepared so that even if you were attacked in the middle of the movement, you would be able to respond instantly. Karate has always stressed the importance of quick and slow, hard and soft elements in its techniques. In punching, the speed of the fist as it leaves the hip and its speed as it travels toward the target are not the same. The fist should be travelling fastest at the instant it strikes. Thus, even in a punch executed as quickly as possible, there are faster and slower phases. This second movement is to be executed slowly, and there is a similar variation in speed. To further understand this movement and its finer points, it is best to experiment yourself. I am sure that you will discover many important points.

3. Take a large step forward with the left leg into a left front stance, while pulling the right fist to the right side and thrusting the left fist straight ahead at the level of the solar plexus (fig. 6). At the moment of focus let go with a vigorous kiai.

The only difference from step 1 above is that you are punching with your left hand. A review of the chapter on stances is advisable to grasp anew the main points.

4. Retract the left foot, lower the fists and return to the yōi posture (fig. 7).

This concludes the explanation of the first movement of Ten no Kata Omote, chūdan oi-zuki. Naturally, it is all right to practice this movement several times before going on to the next movement.

3   4

5   6   7

B. UPPER LEVEL THRUST PUNCH   *Jōdan Oi-zuki*

1. From yōi posture, step forward with the right leg into a right front stance. At the same time, pull the left fist back to the left side, and thrust the right fist to the face level (figs. 8–9). Do not forget to give a kiai.

The only difference from chūdan oizuki is that the punch is to the upper level, here, the face in general. A specific target is the spot located just below the nose and just above the upper lip. Imagine your opponent is exactly your height and aim your punch accordingly. Not having an actual target, your fist may tend to wander to the right, ending up above your opponent's left shoulder. Be especially careful to punch directly toward the middle. Otherwise, this practice is meaningless.

A bad habit of beginners when punching to the upper level is raising their shoulders. When the shoulders are raised, power escapes from under the arms, and the fist tends to travel in an arc. Another problem that often plagues beginners is that the shoulder on the punching side extends ahead of the body, throwing the upper body off balance. When this happens, not only are you unable to deliver an effective attack, but you are extremely vulnerable to counterat-

8

9

tack. The beginner may deem it unnecessary to think this far ahead, but those who practice the martial arts always have an ultimate ideal in mind. One should try to approach that ideal, little by little, in every practice.

2. Retract the right foot, lower the fists and return to the yōi posture (fig. 10).

3. Take a large step forward with the left leg into a left front stance while pulling the right fist back to the right side and punching to the upper level with the left fist (fig. 11). At the moment of focus, give a loud, vigorous kiai.

4. Retract the left foot, lower the fists and return to the yōi posture (fig. 12).

10

11

12

C. MIDDLE LEVEL REVERSE PUNCH

Chūdan Gyaku-zuki

1. From the yōi posture take a large step forward with the left leg into the immovable stance. As you step, pull the right fist back once to the right side, then thrust it forward at solar plexus level while simultaneously pulling the left fist back to the left side (figs. 13–14).

Review my previous description of fudō-dachi.

Gyaku-zuki is a technique unique to karate, and therefore it is essential to practice it assiduously. To tell the truth, you will not be able to step and punch at exactly the same time; the step will be a shade faster. Stepping forward with the left leg, twist your hips as you pull your right fist back to the side. Then as your left foot touches the floor, thrust your right fist forward. At the instant of punching, your hips must be very low.

13

14

2. Retract the left foot to the starting position, lower the fists and return to the yōi posture (fig. 15).

3. Take a large step forward with the right leg into the immovable stance and pull the left hand back to the left side for an instant. Then thrust it forward in a middle level punch while simultaneously pulling back the right hand (fig. 16).

Bend the knees deeply and maintain firm control of your legs. Punch while twisting the hips.

4. Retract the right leg, lower the fists and return to the yōi posture (fig. 17).

D. UPPER LEVEL
REVERSE PUNCH

1. Take a large step forward with the left leg into the immovable stance. Pull the right fist back to the right side for an instant, then thrust it forward to the upper level while simultaneously pulling the left fist back (figs. 18–19).

Just as in the upper level thrust punch, make sure that the shoulders are not raised and that the attacking fist travels in a straight line directly to the target.

2. Retract the left foot to its original position while slowly lowering the fists and returning to the yōi position (fig. 20).

3. Take a large step forward with the right leg into the immovable stance. Pull the left fist back to the left side for an instant, then thrust it forward toward the upper level while simultaneously pulling back the right fist (fig. 21).

18

19

4. Retract the right foot while lowering the fists, and return to the yōi position (fig. 22).

The above four movements constitute basic practice in karate punching. The regular fist is used throughout. Five or ten minutes should be sufficient to learn these four movements, but never forget that developing a truly effective punch will take great effort and hundreds of thousands of repetitions.

20

21

22

E. DOWN BLOCK
MIDDLE LEVEL
REVERSE PUNCH

Gedan-barai
Chūdan Gyaku-zuki

1. From the yōi posture, step back with the right leg into the immovable stance. Pull the right fist back to the right side, and strike down diagonally with the left fist, starting from a position in front of the right shoulder (figs. 23–24).

This action is meant to block a punch to the lower level. Step back to gain the proper distance and strike with the left arm, hitting the opponent's hand with your wrist and sweeping it obliquely. To add force to the block, raise your left fist to a position in front of your right shoulder with the back of the fist downward, then swing it down, rotating the fist at the moment of focus so that the back of the fist comes upward. The left fist should stop at a position about seventeen to twenty centimeters above the bent left knee. Lower both shoulders, keep the chin pulled in, and stare directly into the eyes of your imaginary opponent. The upper body should be in the half-front-facing posture but with the right fist fully pulled back to the right hip, the body may face almost completely sideways.

2. Pull the left fist back to the left side while simultaneously thrusting the right fist forward in a middle level attack (fig. 25). Give a vigorous kiai at the moment of focus. This holds true for all the following movements.

Make sure that in punching from the immovable stance the legs maintain the correct form. The key points of the punch are exactly the same as those for the middle level reverse punch. Be especially careful not to raise the hips.

3. Return to the yōi posture by slowly bringing the right foot forward and lowering the fists (fig. 26).

4. Draw the left leg back while making a down block with the right fist and simultaneously pulling the left fist back to the hip (fig. 27).

5. Pull the right fist back to the right side. Give a good kiai and thrust the left fist forward in a middle level attack (fig. 28).

6. Slowly bring the left foot forward and lower the fists to return to the yōi posture (fig. 29).

Practice the block-attack combinations (A–B, C–D) as two separate actions to ensure that you do them correctly and with full strength. However, you must already be attacking at the instant of your block, so the combinations must eventually be performed as a single continuous action. This is also true for all the following movements.

23

24

25

26

27

28

29

F. MIDDLE LEVEL INSIDE FOREARM BLOCK MIDDLE LEVEL REVERSE PUNCH

Chūdan Ude Uke

Chūdan Gyaku-zuki

1. From the yōi posture, step back with the right leg into the immovable stance. Starting from in front of the right shoulder, swing the left fist in an arc across the body, using the half-bent left elbow as a pivot (figs. 30–31). Simultaneously pull the right fist back to the right side.

Use your wrist as though to hit and sweep the opponent's punch to your chest. When the left fist is brought in front of the right shoulder, the back of the fist should be upward. Swing the fist in an arc, and at the instant of contact with his punching hand, rotate the wrist so that the back of the fist comes downward. Catch and sweep aside his wrist with the area below the base of the thumb of your blocking arm. At the end of the block, your fist should be at shoulder height in a position above your left knee.

30   31

2. Pull the left fist back to the left side while executing a middle level punch with the right fist and two kiai (fig. 32).

3. Slowly bring the right foot forward and lower the fists to return to the yōi posture (fig. 33).

4. Step back with the left foot into the immovable stance. Block with the right arm by bringing the fist from the left shoulder to a position in front of the right shoulder with the elbow half-bent (fig. 34). At the same time, pull the left fist back to the left side.

5. Pull the right fist back to the right side and make a middle level punch with the left fist (fig. 35).

6. Return to the yōi posture (fig. 36).

32

33

34

35

36

G. MIDDLE LEVEL SWORD HAND BLOCK MIDDLE LEVEL SPEAR HAND ATTACK

Chūdan Shutō Uke

Chūdan Nukite

1. Step back with the right foot into the back stance. Starting from in front of the right shoulder, strike with the sword hand sweeping toward the front while keeping the left elbow bent (figs. 37–38). Simultaneously position the right arm in front of the chest. The sword hand is explained in the chapter on hand techniques. In making the sword hand be sure that the thumb is folded; otherwise it can be easily caught and injured in your opponent's sleeve, or even in his hand.

When the left hand is brought back to a position in front of the right shoulder, the back of the hand is down. With the elbow acting as a pivot, the blocking hand accelerates as it travels in an arc. A split second before the moment of contact, the wrist is rotated so the back of the hand comes up.

Although the back stance resembles the immovable stance, you should have the feeling of putting your entire weight on the back leg and having the front leg only lightly touching the ground. The main feature of shutō is that the side of the hand is used like a sword. You should practice with the aim of diagonally slicing off your opponent's hand. The fingertips of the blocking hand should be level with your shoulders.

37   38   39

2. Make a fist with the left hand while pulling it to the left side. At the same time make a spear hand with the right hand and thrust it forward in a middle level attack (fig. 39). Kiai at this point.

Refer again to the chapter on hand techniques. Think of the extended fingertips of the spear hand as a dagger and thrust them forward into the opponent's solar plexus. The palm of the hand faces to the left. Lower the shoulders, and do not forget to tighten the underarm muscles.

40   41

42   43

3. Return the right foot to the original starting position and slowly lower the hands, thus returning to the yōi posture (fig. 40).

4. Step back with the left leg into the back stance. Pull the left fist back to the left side and with the right hand block to the front with the sword hand (fig. 41).

5. Make a fist with the right hand and pull it back to the hip while delivering a middle level spear hand attack with the left hand (fig. 42).

6. Return the left foot to the original starting position and slowly lower the hands, thus returning to the yōi posture (fig. 43).

H. UPPER LEVEL SWORD HAND SWEEP   *Jōdan Shutō-barai*
UPPER LEVEL THRUST   *Jōdan-zuki*

1. From the yōi posture step back with the right foot into the immovable stance. Pull the right fist back to the right side while simultaneously making a sword hand with the left hand. With the elbow bent and acting as a pivot, swing the left hand upward in an arc to block at eye level (figs. 44–45).

44   45

This movement uses the wrist to block an upper level attack. Despite the fact that *shutō-barai* means "sword hand sweep," the aim here is to hit and stop the opponent's attacking hand, rather than sweep it away or slice it off as in the sword hand block.

2. Make a fist with the left hand and pull it back to the left side while simultaneously executing an upper level attack with the right fist and a kiai (fig. 46).

Strike with the aim of grabbing your opponent's wrist with your blocking hand and pulling it to your hip. As you break his stance and balance by pulling his arm, deliver an attack to the point just below his nose with your right fist.

3. Bring the right foot forward to the original starting position and lower the hands to return to the yōi posture (fig. 47).

4. Step back with the left foot into the immovable stance and pull the left fist back to the left side while executing an upper level block with the right sword hand (fig. 48).

5. Make a fist with the right hand and pull it back to the right side while delivering a left upper level attack (fig. 49). Give a kiai.

6. Bring the left foot forward to the original starting position and lower the hands to return to the yōi posture (fig. 50).

46

47

48

49

50

I. UPPER LEVEL RISING BLOCK   *Jōdan Age-uke*
MIDDLE LEVEL   *Chūdan Gyaku-zuki*
REVERSE PUNCH

1. Step back with the right leg into the immovable stance while pulling the right fist back to the right side and raising the left arm in a rising block as shown in the diagram (figs. 51–52). The back of the fist should be toward the forehead with the little finger uppermost.

Block with the aim of snapping the opponent's attacking arm up from below. As shown in the diagram, the area of contact is on the ulna (little finger) side of the forearm. The back of your left hand should be twelve to fifteen centimeters from your forehead. You should be looking at your opponent from just below your raised fist. The elbow should be held somewhat vertically and should be low enough to guard your rib cage.

The most important point is to make sure that you block with your whole body. If you block an opponent who's your equal with your wrist only, you will simply be overpowered. In other words, while thrusting your blocking hand upward, you must lower your hips. Your upper body should never lean backwards; in fact, there is an advantage in leaning slightly forward.

51   52

2. Pull the left fist back to the left side while countering with a middle level reverse punch with the right fist (fig. 53). Give a kiai.

3. Bring the right foot to the original starting position and lower the fists to return to the yōi posture (fig. 54).

4. Step back with the left foot into the immovable stance while pulling the left fist back to the left side and raising the right fist above the forehead (fig. 55).

5. Pull the right fist back to the right side while countering with a middle level reverse punch using the left hand (fig. 56). Give a kiai.

6. Return to the yōi posture (fig. 57).

53

54

55

56

57

J. UPPER LEVEL IRON HAMMER BLOCK MIDDLE LEVEL ATTACK

Jōdan Uchikomi

Chūdan-zuki

1. From the yōi posture step back with the right leg into the immovable stance. After first raising the left fist high above the head, strike diagonally downward in front of the eyes. At the same time, pull the right fist back to the right side.

Raise your blocking fist with the back toward you. As you swing it downward, rotate the wrist so that the back of the fist is now away from you. At the end of the block, your fist should be slightly below eye level and about forty centimeters from your face. As your opponent attacks your face, you should counter as though to break his arm with your wrist or iron hammer. Strike downward in a slightly diagonal path. It is normal for the fist to be in a slightly more forward position than for a middle level inside forearm block.

58

59

2. Pull the left fist back to the left side and at the same time execute a middle level attack with the right hand (fig. 60). Give a kiai.

3. Bring the right foot back to the original starting position and lower the fists to return to the yōi posture (fig. 61).

4. Step back with the left leg into the immovable stance. Raise the right fist high above your head, then strike down diagonally in front of the eyes while pulling the left fist back to the left side (fig. 62).

5. Pull the right fist back to the right side while attacking to the middle level with the left fist and letting out a kiai (fig. 63).

6. Bring the left foot back to the original starting position and lower the fists, thus returning to the yōi posture (fig. 64).

At the command of *Yame*, "Stop," first move the left foot inward and then the right. Stand at attention, and bow respectfully at the command of *Rei*, "Bow." This ends the kata.

60

61

62

63

64

12: TEN NO KATA URA

Ten no Kata Ura consists of the six movements in Ten no Kata Omote that involve blocking, that is, movements E–J, practiced with a real opponent. As I explained earlier, in karate-dō this form of practice is called kumite.

In the illustrations that follow, the person on the right is the attacker, and the person on the left is the defender. In actual practice the partners take turns alternating roles. The attacker always starts from a gedan-barai posture and attacks with oi-zuki. In studying the movements, pay special attention to the explanations in the previous chapter so that the key points can be grasped.

The attacker should always let out a vigorous kiai at the instant of attack. The defender should do the same with his counterattack. In letting out a kiai, you must exert sufficient strength in the *tanden*, the center of gravity in the lower abdomen, and have the feeling of spiritually besting your opponent. At first, the defender should practice his block and counterattack as two separate techniques. As he becomes more adept, he should execute the two in one action so that not even a split second elapses between block and counterattack.

A. DOWNWARD BLOCK
MIDDLE LEVEL PUNCH

Gedan-barai
Chūdan-zuki

Before beginning this practice, both men face the front of the dojo and bow respectfully. Then they face and bow to each other (figs. 1–2). The distance between them should be about 1.8 meters.

1. At the command of Yōi, the attacker steps forward with his left foot into the front stance, his left arm held in the downward block position and his right hand held at his hip. He must look directly into the defender's eyes.

The defender takes the open leg *shizentai*, ''natural,'' stance, which is the yōi posture for the Omote section of the kata. He too should look directly into his partner's eyes and be mentally prepared for an attack at any moment (fig. 3).

At the count of *ichi*, ''one,'' the attacker steps in and executes a lower level right front punch and a kiai while pulling his left fist back to his left side (fig. 4).

1

2

3

4

The defender steps back with his right foot and uses his left arm to block the attacker's wrist with a downward block while pulling his right hand back to his hip (fig. 5).

2. At the count of *ni*, ''two,'' the attacker stands motionless with his eyes fixed on the defender's eyes.

The defender pulls his left hand back to his left hip while simultaneously executing a right middle level reverse punch and a kiai (fig. 6).

3. At the count of *san*, ''three,'' the attacker pulls his right foot back and returns to the yōi posture.

The defender brings his right foot forward into the yōi posture. The distance between partners should now be about 90 centimeters (fig. 7).

5

7

1. At the command of Yōi, the attacker steps back with his left leg into a right front stance. His left fist is at his hip and his right fist is in the downward block position.

8   9

The defender does not move (figs. 8–9).

At the count of ichi, the attacker steps in with his left foot and executes a lower level punch. Kiai at this point.

The defender steps back with his left foot and executes a downward block with his right fist while pulling his left fist back to his hip (fig. 10).

2. At the count of ni, the attacker does not move.

The defender pulls his right fist to his hip and with his left fist executes a middle level reverse punch. Kiai at this point (fig. 11).

3. At the count of san, the attacker brings his left foot back and slowly lowers his fists and returns to the yōi posture.

The defender brings his left foot forward and returns to the yōi posture (fig. 12).

These right and left punches are executed exactly as in the first two movements of the Omote section of the kata. The attacker must make a determined effort to step in fully and thrust his fist forward with the intention of really penetrating his partner. If he does not do so, it will be more difficult for the defender to make a good block. Furthermore, the attacker must practice attacking strongly enough so that even though his fist is swept aside, he does not lose his balance or stance. The defender should have the confidence to block and sweep away any attack, regardless of its strength. After completion of this movement, the attacker and the defender should change roles.

The following movements are defenses against a right front punch.

10

11

12

B. MIDDLE LEVEL INSIDE FOREARM BLOCK MIDDLE LEVEL PUNCH

Chūdan Ude Uke

Chūdan-zuki

Yōi (fig. 13).

Attacker: Step back with the right leg into the left front stance. Hold the left fist in downward block position and pull the right fist to the right side.

Defender: Take the yōi posture (fig. 14).

1. Attacker: Take a large step forward with the right leg and execute a middle level attack while pulling the left fist to the left side. Kiai at this point.

Defender: Step back with the right leg into the immovable stance and use the left fist to strike the opponent's wrist to the outside while pulling the right fist back to the right side. Kiai at this point (fig. 15).

13

14

15

2. Attacker: Do not move.

Defender: Pull the left fist back to the left side while executing a middle level attack with the right fist. Kiai at this point (fig. 16).

3. Attacker: Pull the right leg back and return to the yōi posture.

Defender: Step forward with the right leg and return to the yōi posture (fig. 17).

In movements 4–6, attacker and defender repeat the above movements using the opposite hand and leg (figs. 18–20).

16

17

18

19

20

C. MIDDLE LEVEL SWORD HAND BLOCK   *Chūdan Shutō Uke*
MIDDLE LEVEL PUNCH   *Chūdan-zuki*

Yōi (fig. 21).

Attacker: Step back with the right foot into the left front stance. Hold the left fist in the downward block position.

Defender: Take the yōi posture (fig. 22).

1. Attacker: Take a large step forward with the right leg and execute a middle level attack with the right fist. Kiai at this point.

Defender: Step back with the right leg into the back stance. Pull the right hand to the side while simultaneously cutting and sweeping the opponent's wrist diagonally toward the outside with the left sword hand (fig. 23).

21

22

23

2. Attacker: Do not move.

Defender: Make a fist with the left hand and pull it to the left side while opening the right fist and executing a middle level spear hand attack (fig. 24).

3. Attacker: Pull the right leg back and return to the yōi posture (fig. 25).

24

25

Defender: Step up with the right leg and return to the yōi posture.

In movements 4–6, attacker and defender repeat the above movements using the opposite hand and leg (figs. 26–28).

26

27

28

D. UPPER LEVEL SWORD HAND SWEEP UPPER LEVEL PUNCH

Jōdan Shutō-barai

Jōdan-zuki

Yōi (fig. 29).

Attacker: Step back with the right leg into the left front stance and hold the left fist in the downward block position.

Defender: Take the yōi posture (fig. 30).

1. Attacker: Take a large step forward with the right leg and execute an upper level punch with the right fist. Kiai at this point.

Defender: Step back with the right leg into the immovable stance and pull the right fist to the right side while using the left sword hand to block the opponent's wrist (fig. 31).

29

30

31

2. Attacker: Do not move.

Defender: With the left hand, grab the opponent's wrist and twist it as you pull it toward you while executing an upper level attack with the right fist. Kiai at this point (fig. 32).

3. Attacker: Pull the right leg back and return to the yōi posture.

Defender: Step up with the right leg, release the opponent's wrist and return to the yōi posture (fig. 33).

In movements 4–6, attacker and defender repeat the above movements using the opposite hand and leg (figs. 34–36).

32

34

33

35

36

E. UPPER LEVEL RISING BLOCK   *Jōdan Age-uke*
MIDDLE LEVEL PUNCH   *Chūdan-zuki*

Yōi (fig. 37).

Attacker: Step back with the right leg into the front stance. Pull the right fist to the side and hold the left fist in the downward block position.

Defender: Take the yōi posture (fig. 38).

1. Attacker: Step forward with the right leg and execute an upper level punch. Kiai at this point.

Defender: Step back with the right leg into the immovable stance. Pull the right fist to the right side while using the left wrist to snap the opponent's attacking hand upward (fig. 39).

2. Attacker: Do not move.

Defender: Pull the left fist back to the left side and execute a middle level attack with the right fist. Kiai at this point (fig. 40).

37

38

39

40

3. Attacker: Pull the right leg back and return to the yōi posture.

Defender: Step up with the right leg and return to the yōi posture (fig. 41).

In movements 4–6, attacker and defender repeat the above steps using the opposite hand and leg (figs. 42–44).

41

42

43

44

F. UPPER LEVEL HAMMER BLOCK MIDDLE LEVEL PUNCH

Jōdan Uchikomi

Chūdan-zuki

Yōi (fig. 45).

Attacker: Step back with the right leg into the left front stance and hold the left fist in the downward block position.

Defender: Take the yōi posture (fig. 46).

1. Attacker: Take a large step forward with the right leg and execute an upper level attack with the right fist. Pull the left fist to left side.

Defender: Step back with the right leg into the immovable stance. Pull the right fist to the right side and simultaneously swing the left fist upward. Using the iron hammer or the wrist of the left hand, strike the opponent's arm diagonally downward (fig. 47).

2. Attacker: Do not move.

Defender: Pull the left fist back to the left side and execute a middle level attack with the right fist. Kiai at this point (fig. 48).

45

46

47

48

3. Attacker: Pull the right leg back and return to the yōi posture.

Defender: Step forward with the right leg and return to the yōi posture (fig. 49).

In movements 4–6, attacker and defender repeat the above steps using the opposite hand and leg (figs. 50–52).

After the completion of these movements, the partners should exchange roles.

Except for the last one, all of the blocks described here are inside blocks. The opponent's attacking arm is swept from the inside outward. The last one, the upper level hammer block, is an outside block in which the attacking arm is struck from the outside inward.

Inside blocks can be made into outside blocks by switching the stepping leg and blocking hand. Therefore, if attacked with a right punch, step back with the left leg and block with the right hand and vice versa.

Rei.

Once again, at a distance of about 1.8 meters, the partners bow to each other. Then turning to face the front of the dojo, they bow once more.

This concludes Ten no Kata Ura.

49

50

51

52

13: VIGNETTES OF THREE TEACHERS

One of the village elders announced the village headman's order in his loudest voice: all young men were to assemble in the village square. Such a summons was a rare occurrence, and could only mean that the headman of Azato Village, Azato Yasutsune, had something of great importance to impart.

Master Azato, peerless warrior that he was, excelled in stick techniques, swordsmanship, horsemanship—all the martial arts in fact. Among the men who looked up to him with respect was the great karate master, Itosu Yasutsune himself.

With a man like that to inspire them, it was natural for the young men of the village to take easily to the martial arts. Every evening after work, they practiced sumo in the village square. The square was also the scene of weight-lifting contests and stick training; they fairly made the twilight air whistle with their staff and stick attacks. Quarrels and confrontations among youths boastful of their prowess were not infrequent, and inevitably these sometimes led to serious matches. Even the number of times a man had simply been to the square could become a matter of pride because of the valuable experience that was to be gained there.

As they now assembled, these stalwart young men with outstanding physiques were a sight to behold.

Master Azato, receiving word that all were present, stepped forward with an air of perfect composure.

It was said that when he got angry, his eyes could make even a tiger cower. Today, he smiled good-naturedly as he said, "First of all, thank you for coming. Please come closer, for I have something I want you to hear, and it's important that I tell all of you. Are you sure no one's absent?"

Slowly he surveyed the faces around him and said, "Just a minute, it seems that someone is missing. Who can it be?"

A voice spoke up, "Sir, this is everyone—well, anyway, everyone who can move. Kinjō Jirō's not here because he's laid up in bed."

"Oh, that won't do. I insist that he be here. If he can't walk, send my palanquin to bring him here."

Two of the men got up and set out with the palanquin. Ignoring Jirō's cries of protest, they soon returned with him. Slowly, he crawled out of the palanquin, a strapping youth with his head wrapped in a white towel. Despite his brawn, he looked utterly listless and dispirited. The young men who had gone to fetch him reached down to take hold of his arms, but they stopped when Jirō screamed in pain.

Looking on this scene, Master Azato smiled broadly. "Jirō," he asked in a low tone, "what happened to all the energy and spirit you had last night?"

Jirō's eyes flashed in shocked surprise. That voice! He had heard that strong, deep voice before—a voice that sent shivers down the spine and penetrated to the pit of the stomach. "Master, . . ."

"Are you in pain? I guess the medicine might have been a little strong. But listen, Jirō, you're not the only one to feel pain after being hit. You have to know the pain that others feel. You're lucky it was me. If it had been someone like Master Itosu, you'd be crippled for life. I'm sure you've heard of the drunkard who had his fists crushed when he tried to attack Itosu.

"When people heard innocent passersby were being waylaid near the pine grove, they were afraid to go there after dark. Striking down or hurting others is not the goal in practicing our art. Our sole intention is to improve ourselves. I want everyone to listen very carefully, for it seems Jirō is not the only one who has misunderstood. To allow overzealousness or impetuosity to drive one to rash actions is the greatest shame for a samurai. Before using others to test your fists on, first polish your mind and heart."

The village headman addressed the young men with the strictness of a father, but his eyes were filled with a mother's tenderness. After his talk, it is said that rowdy violence among the youths came to a sudden and complete halt.

When Master Azato's son and I studied under Master Itosu, I arose every morning while it was still dark and walked the four kilometers to Itosu's house. Practice finished, I would return home just as people were waking up. I did this diligently every day for ten years and was taught the three Tekki Kata, which were Master Itosu's specialty. I spent over three years on each one, although committing the movements to memory takes only twenty to thirty minutes. This exemplifies the strictness of instruction in olden times. Itosu himself used to say, "The easiest kata to learn are the Tekki but the most difficult kata to learn are also the Tekki."

Itosu had a natural genius for karate-dō. It is said that he created the five Heian Kata. Among the things he was wont to say was, "If one feels no pain when struck, one can disregard the blows," and in fact the blows he could absorb would have floored almost everyone else. This stood in sharp contrast to Azato's oft-quoted "think of the hands and feet as swords."

After drinking, he was apt to turn to the younger students and say, "All right, I'm not going to move. Come and try out your attacks. You can hit me anywhere but the tip of my nose," adding with a laugh, "That's the only place I can't make stronger." There was, however, another thing he was careful about. When out walking at night, he would tuck his long beard into his upper garment. He was very proud of his beard but admitted good-naturedly, "It wouldn't do to let someone grab hold of it."

His great strength and ability not withstanding, he never ceased polishing his art. There were times when even Azato was struck with wonder and admiration at the awesome power of Itosu's fist. Once the two were drinking together when they decided to go visit the home of a certain man. On arriving, they found the large front gate barred from the inside. At first they thought that no one was home, but then they caught the boisterous sounds of a lively drinking session going on inside. Still, no matter how loudly they knocked and called out, their arrival went unnoticed.

Finally, Master Azato said, "Itosu, this looks hopeless. Shall we go home?" But Master Itosu answered, "Wait a minute. I'll open the gate."

His drinking couldn't have improved his aim, but it seems to have lowered his natural inhibitions against inflicting property damage. After approximating the location of the bar, he let go with a tremendous kiai and promptly a fist-sized hole appeared in the eighteen-centimeter-thick wooden wall. Itosu withdrew his fist, then reached back in, unhooked the bar, and the two karate masters walked nonchalantly through the gate. Azato's only comment was, "That's a terrific fist." He must have been deeply impressed, though, for he often repeated the story.

There is a story about Matsumura Sensei, one of the greatest karate experts of all times, and how he defeated a certain Uehara in a match without striking a blow. The tale has the flavor of a legend, but I would like to tell it here anyway.

"Aren't you Matsumura Sensei?" The metal craftsman named Uehara was addressing the young man who had come into his shop to ask for the metal ends of his tobacco pipe to be changed. Uehara, in the prime of his life, was a man of forty-two or forty-three. He had a ruddy complexion, his eyebrows were set well up on his high broad forehead, and the top of his freshly-shaven head was bluish green. His neck was as thick as a bull's, while his clothes concealed thickly muscled shoulders, a huge chest and thick brawny arms. Surprisingly, his eyes were soft like those of a small child, and the corners crinkled as he sat on his work mat smiling up at his visitor.

The young man appeared to be about twenty-seven or twenty-eight, certainly not more than thirty. His sharp piercing eyes gave off a penetrating glare. He was quite tall, probably about 180 centimeters or so, but on the thin side. An unfathomable energy flowed from that long lanky body, but his color was not good, showing signs of a pale green pallor.

Around his forehead there appeared to hang an undefined shadow; in general, though, he looked to be a man of good social standing. He had about him the dignified air of a government official.

Hearing his name asked, he scowled, drew his brows together and answered tersely, "Yes. So?" He fixed his piercing gaze on the craftsman's face, as if looking for some deeper meaning behind the seemingly innocent inquiry.

Avoiding Matsumura's eyes, the craftsman reached for the pipe. Inspecting it as he slowly turned it in the palm of his hand, he said, "So, you are Matsumura, the karate master. Actually, I've been looking for a chance to meet you. I've been hoping to ask you to instruct me in karate."

"Sorry, I'm not a karate instructor."

"If you are not the karate instructor, then who is it that's teaching the lord of the castle? There is no other instructor as accomplished and as famous as you," he said. Then with a mischievous grin that seemed to say, "Try to talk your way out of this," the craftsman raised his eyes to return Matsumura's glare.

With a look of great displeasure Matsumura replied, "I was the lord's karate instructor, but someone else will take my place. I quit. To tell the truth, I'm disgusted with it all, especially karate!"

Still looking directly into the young man's eyes, Uehara said, "Well, now, that sounds rather strange. The minister of military affairs, the great Matsumura Sensei of whom the lord of the castle is so fond, has for some reason or another become disgusted with karate. If it's come to that, you can't very well carry out your official duties."

"I don't have any duties," shot back Matsumura. "Carrying out my duties landed me in a lot of trouble."

"The more I hear, the more confused I get," countered the older man. "I do not wish to sound disrespectful, but among those left at the castle, there is no one of any real ability. If you won't teach our lord, who can?"

"That's how things got out of hand. His techniques are still immature. He still has a long way to go. He must polish himself a lot more—reach a much higher level. Oh, I could lose to him easily enough, but that wouldn't help him at all. I scolded him, taunted him, asked if he really thought his attacks would be effective against an actual opponent. Furious, but deadly serious, he

102

jumped at my head with a double kick. The kicks were strong, no denying that, but to suddenly jump in with a double kick against a stronger opponent is a sign of insufficient training.

"Ridiculous, I thought to myself, but I decided to take advantage of the opportunity to teach our lord a well deserved lesson. A karate match should be no different from a match with real swords. There's no room to think, 'If I fail, I can try again.' Such an attitude is incompatible with true practice. Unfortunately, our lord always approached practice with this attitude.

"I decided to give him a taste of the consequences when one fails. That's why I let him have it. I hit the leg aimed at my head with my sword hand, then I swept away his second kicking leg with a forearm block. He was about to fall flat on his side when I hit him once more with a body blow, sending him flying. He landed about six meters away. . ."

Uehara's eyes were opened wide with amazement. "That sounds like a pretty rough session. Was our lordship hurt?"

Without a trace of emotion, Matsumura said, "Yes. His shoulder, where he landed; his hand. The leg I hit was badly swollen. I don't think he was able to get up."

"Whew, you really let him have it, didn't you? But of course, you were reprimanded?"

"That goes without saying—and more severely than you might expect. I was told to get out and to stay out until further notice."

"I don't doubt it," said Uehara, nodding his head. "But of course, it probably won't be long before you're called back and all is forgiven."

"I don't think so. Our lord is beside himself with anger. It's already been one hundred days and still no word. Someone told me our lord said, 'Matsumura is extremely proud of his moderate skill.' I don't expect I'll ever be forgiven. It would have been better if I'd never taken up teaching karate, better yet if I'd never learned it!"

"That's a pretty weak-hearted way to look at it," said Uehara as he leaned forward. "Lived in anger, lived in laughter—a lifetime is still a lifetime. What do you say—why don't you favor me with a lesson? It may chase away your gloom."

Matsumura's eyes flared for just an instant. "No lessons. Besides, you yourself are a well-known martial artist. People call you 'Karate' Uehara. Why do you need a lesson from me?"

"It's not a matter of necessity," replied Uehara calmly. "I felt it would be interesting to see at firsthand the teaching methods of a famous instructor."

Considering the difference in social standing between the two men, the craftsman's language was respectful, but there was a glint in his eyes that betrayed a quite different attitude. Even though

Uehara was well known as a karate expert in the Naha and Shuri districts, it would never have been possible for him to study under the instructor to the lord of the castle. Yet he was telling Matsumura to show him his skills, as if he were ordering a student to perform.

Young, excitable, Matsumura read the intent in Uehara's eyes and was incensed. "Are you deaf! I've already said I've stopped giving lessons."

"All right, I can see you aren't going to instruct me, so how about granting me a match?"

"A match—you're challenging me to a match?"

"That's right. In the martial arts there's no difference between rich and poor, high and low. And remember, you're no longer the official instructor, so there's no need for any official permission. Please rest assured I have no intention of letting a foolish kick end up in a swollen leg, or a clumsy fall injure my hand."

When Matsumura failed to reply, Uehara pressed on, "Something wrong? You have my word; I don't intend to be rough or violent, and I won't cause you to suffer any serious injuries."

Matsumura glared at his challenger. "Uehara, I don't know how good you are in karate, but you should be more careful with your tongue! As for your challenge, a match is a matter of life and death. There is no room for concern about whether or not one gets hurt. There can be no crying or complaining. I assume you understand that."

"Of course, it's exactly as you say. All along, I've been totally prepared to accept the consequences. How about you, Sensei?"

"All right, I'll grant you your wish. One can never predict the outcome of a match. It's said that when two tigers fight, one is always wounded, the other surely dies. Win or lose, don't expect to come out of this intact. I'll leave the time and place up to you."

Uehara's tone suddenly became formal. "I deeply appreciate your speedy acceptance of my challenge. Then by your leave, let me set the time of the match at 5:00 A.M. tomorrow. The place will be the Kinbu Palace graveyard."

After Matsumura left, Uehara began to slowly clean up his workshop while busily mulling the situation. Matsumura's still young, he thought, but he looks very capable. I wonder how good he really is. Nothing wrong with his reputation, but from the way he treated our lord, it's obvious he's got a hot temper. Should I bait him and provoke him? No, he's not so immature or inexperienced as to fall for that. The only thing to do is to seize the initiative: jump in and press home my attack. Feeling rather satisfied with his tentative decision, Uehara noticed that his shoulders had become very tight. He decided to loosen them up.

He finished tidying up and strolled outside. Turning to face his shop, he stared up at the eaves for a moment. Then, with a light spring, he was suddenly off the ground and gripping the end of a rafter with his fingertips. He looked as if he were swinging from a crossbar in a gym. With an easy swing of his body, he released one hand and reached out and grabbed the next rafter. Repeating the motion, he moved to the next, and then to the next. Swinging in this monkey-like fashion, he smoothly made several rounds of the building. He dropped to the ground just as dusk was falling, and bats were starting to dot the evening sky.

The lone figure of a man made its way up the slope to the Kinbu Palace graveyard. Fresh morning air filled his lungs, and the dew drops clinging to the grass drenched the hem of his robe as he walked. The figure was ''Karate'' Uehara. It was still a little before sunrise when he arrived, and the graveyard was cloaked in semidarkness. ''It must be just past four. It'll be some time before Matsumura arrives. I might as well relax and settle down. Think I'll have a smoke.''

Searching the open space in the graveyard for a place to sit, his head suddenly came to an abrupt halt. He had not noticed it before, but there in the faint shadows of a stand of trees, on a large rock amid the tall grass, sat a figure, steadily staring in his direction. Unsure, he asked, ''Matsumura Sensei?''

''That's right. You're early aren't you?''

''So are you; you're very early. You caught me by surprise.''

''Then it must not take very much to surprise you. I'm ready whenever you are. Or would you rather wait until five o'clock?''

''Yes, well, either way is fine with me, but please, let me have a smoke first.''

Sitting down at the base of large tree, Uehara removed his pipe from his waistband. Savoring the taste of the tobacco, he began to take deep puffs, watching the rings of violet smoke rise and vanish in the crystal morning air. In the trees, he could hear the gentle melodies of the small birds singing to one another. For a long moment, he enjoyed the idyllic scene.

Finally, Uehara tapped the ashes out of his pipe, and very carefully, almost lovingly, slipped it back into his waistband. He stood up and said, ''Well, I guess we should get started.''

''Fine,'' said Matsumura, rising quickly.

The two men were separated by some nine to ten meters. In a rapid shuffling motion, Uehara quickly closed the distance by about half. He lowered his hips, his left fist held in a downward block position and his right fist at his hip. From there he studied his opponent's stance.

Matsumura was still in the posture he had taken when he first stood up. His left leg was slightly forward but otherwise it seemed an ordinary natural stance—except for his head. His chin was tucked tightly against his left shoulder and his fierce eyes were opened wider than usual.

Uehara felt a tinge of doubt. What was the man up to? Was that his ready position? Matsumura was said to be a great master, but Uehara had a reputation to be proud of too. For Matsumura to stand in such an awkward posture when facing Uehara could mean only one thing: unimaginable confidence. Either that or he was out of his mind. Uehara decided there was only one way to find out— charge in and rout his opponent. But at the instant he made his decision, he felt himself suddenly hit by a flash of purple light seemingly emanating from Matsumura's eyes. Before he knew what he had done, he had retreated three and a half meters.

Looking again at his opponent, Uehara could see Matsumura had not budged. He stood exactly as before. To Uehara's consternation, he discovered his own forehead and armpits were dripping with a greasy sweat and his heart was pounding violently.

"Uehara, is something wrong?"

"I don't know. I feel very strange. Please give me a moment."

Feeling terribly exhausted all of a sudden, Uehara returned to the tree where he had sat earlier and slumped down. Matsumura, composed as ever, once again sat down on his rock.

Uehara's head was full of confused thoughts. What on earth was the matter? Without even fighting, I'm drenched in sweat. And my heart. . .this is strange, very strange. Before he was aware, he had taken out his pipe. He sat there puffing on it slowly. The birds were still singing, but he could no longer hear them. His head hanging, he stared fixedly at the ground.

"Uehara, the sun will be up soon. Aren't you ready yet?"

Without replying, Uehara raised his head and gazed at Matsumura. The contrast with the troubled preoccupied young man who had visited his shop the day before startled him. Matsumura, his face almost beaming, seemed like a different person.

The metal craftsman's thoughts steadied. I should be ashamed of myself. In technique and strategy, I bow to no one, and I have more matches to my credit than anyone else. Will I allow myself to lose to this greenhorn? Fired with spirit, filled with pride, Uehara rose again. "I'm sorry to have made you wait. Shall we try again?"

"Anything you say. Come!" Matsumura assumed the same posture as before, the same defiant glare.

Determined not to fail this time, Uehara steeled himself. Breathing from his lower abdomen, he began to cut the distance between them—nine meters, seven, five, three—just a little closer and then—Uehara couldn't move! It was as if his feet were nailed to the ground. Staring at his opponent he could only see those eyes! Eyes! Fiery, blazing eyes! They seemed as though they were about to come darting out at him. Paralyzed, he felt as though he were being sucked dry by Matsumura's eyes. Yet he was powerless to look away. He felt trapped; if against all odds he managed to look away, something terrible would come flying at him. He was as immobile as a frog sitting entranced before a snake. Unable to see anything but Matsumura's eyes, he had no idea whatsoever where his opponent's hands or feet were, or what they were doing. This is dangerous, an inner voice warned him. I can't do a thing. I'm going to lose!

With no idea of how he would be able to block or escape an attack, Uehara's confidence failed him. Frantically, he summoned up all his strength for a loud kiai. It was his last hope. Reacting to the kiai, Matsumura would either attack or fall back. That reaction would determine the course of Uehara's last desperate attack. But despite the power of Uehara's kiai, Matsumura acted as if he never even heard it. He stood there calmly. Instantly, Uehara jumped back.

"What's wrong, Uehara? Why don't you try to attack? Just shouting doesn't make a match." The slightest hint of a smile crossed Matsumura's lips. He seemed almost cheerful as he looked down on his exhausted opponent.

"This is totally strange. I'm not trying to brag, but no one has ever defeated me in a match before."

"Do you want to stop this match?"

Uehara folded his arms and thought long and hard. At last, with a look of triumph, he raised his head. "Let's continue. I must go on until the match is decided—even though it's already been decided. At any rate, if I let things stand as they are, I'll lose face. My life is no longer of any concern to me. I will try to attack you one last time."

"Fine. If that's what you want, come and try."

Uehara straightened up for a second, made an abrupt bow, and then flew at Matsumura with the energy of a fireball and the will to smash through a massive rock. But the instant before Uehara's bull-like body crashed into his opponent, Matsumura gave off a tremendous shout. In its power and magnitude, it was almost inhuman, reverberating like thunder. Uehara's legs were suddenly seized by cramps, but versed in the Way of the Warrior, he ignored them. With his last ounce of courage, he valiantly tried to press home his attack. But when he looked up at his opponent, he unconsciously let out a gasp and dropped his eyes to the ground.

Like leafy trees atop a towering peak, Matsumura Sensei's hair was blowing wildly in the wind. Behind him the morning sun climbing above the eastern clouds bathed his body in golden flames. With his eyes aglow and mouth wide open, he resembled one of the Five Kings of Light chastizing demons. Little wonder Uehara could not bear to look up. Finally, dropping to his knees, he said from the bottom of his heart, "I've lost. I give up." He placed both hands flat on the ground and bowed.

"What's that? Give up, you say? You, 'Karate' Uehara?"

"I have no excuse. What a fool I was to challenge you. I realize now how poor and unaccomplished I am. I'm totally ashamed of ever having taken pride in being called 'Karate' Uehara."

"Wait! Just as I suspected, your spirit and your skill are truly great. In fact, in technical skill, I have a long way to go before I can equal you."

"What happened, then? What was wrong with me? I couldn't move my hands or feet. I was terrified of your eyes, terrified of your face, of your voice. I could feel no hostility, no fighting spirit—all I felt was fear."

"Perhaps you're right. All along, your mind was filled with the thought of winning, while I was prepared to die. That is the only important difference. Until you challenged me yesterday, I was worried about many things, mainly my position at the castle. But when I made up my mind to accept your challenge, all my troubles suddenly vanished. I realized I'd been allowing myself to become too attached to things, and I was afraid to lose any of them. I was clinging to my skill in karate, and I was clinging to my position as an instructor. I wished to hold onto our lord's affection. I was attached to my personal situation."

"In essence, a man is only a temporary aggregation of the Five Principles and the Five Elements. When his time is up, this form quickly disintegrates, becoming again the elements of earth, water, fire, wind and air. When one realizes the evanescence of all things, it is easy to see that there is no such entity as self, and consequently, no such thing as other. Human beings, like grass or trees, or all of nature, are only physical aggregations of the spirit pervading the entire universe. To the spirit of the universe, the concepts of life and death are meaningless. When one is free of attachment, there are no obstacles or hindrances. There is no fear. That is all."

The story of this match gradually spread, as did word of Uehara's great admiration for Matsumura. First and foremost among the propagators of the story was Uehara himself. He never seemed to tire of telling it to anyone he met, and he never failed to add, "Matsumura is a true master." It is said that before long Matsumura was officially pardoned and returned to his duties at the castle.

Motohiro Yanagisawa, chief of the instruction division of the Shōtōkan (left), demonstrates Kawashi with Junichi Yamamoto

Yasuhiko Suzuki (left) demonstrates Kawashi with Junichi Yamamoto

Yasuaki Hashimoto (left) demonstrates
Kawashi with Noriyuki Terui

Chiharu Yamaki (left) demonstrates
Kawashi with Mikio Inugai

Yoshitake Nakamuta (left) demonstrates
Kawashi with Kuninao Takashima

KUMITE

Age-uke, Gyaku-zuki

Gedan-barai   Gedan-barai

Gedan-zuki

Teisho-zuki

Gedan-zuki

Chūdan-zuki

Chūdan-zuki

Gedan-barai

Chūdan Morote-zuki

Jōdan-zuki

Chūdan-zuki

Chūdan-zuki

Morote-zuki

Morote-zuki

Chūdan Empi Uchi

Chūdan-zuki

Jōdan-zuki

Chūdan-zuki

Jōdan Empi Uchi

Chūdan Empi Uchi

INDEX